God Speaks Navajo

Other Books by Ethel Emily Wallis

Two Thousand Tongues To Go
(with Mary Angela Bennett)
The Dayuma Story
Tariri

≋ God ≋
Speaks
Navajo

BY

Ethel Emily Wallis

NEW YORK, EVANSTON, AND LONDON

Harper & Row, Publishers

1817

FIRST EDITION

LIBRARY OF CONGRESS CATALOG CARD NUMBER: 68-29560

TO
Faith Hill

Contents

Picture section follows p. 82

Preface

NAVAJO INDIANS live in isolated clan settlements scattered over arid stretches of four states, Arizona, New Mexico, Colorado, and Utah. Although now numbering more than one hundred thousand, they are unbelievably unobtrusive, blending harmoniously into a setting of mauve mesas and copper-colored canyons. The People, as they call themselves, constitute a strong minority—the largest tribe of American Indians—and are now in an era of Navajo renaissance. The virility and versatility of their mother tongue, eloquent descendant of ancient Athapaskan, is accountable for much of The People's enduring ethnic strength.

Faye Edgerton formed a part of the Indian landscape where she lived, landlocked, for nearly a half century, identified completely with The People whom she loved. They were her people and she was theirs—because she learned to speak their language. Linked in spirit by this strong bond of communication, she earned the Navajo title, The-One-Who-Understands. And she lert her people an everlasting legacy, the New Testament translated into their own tongue, the beautiful Diné bizaad. But Faye, like Navajos hidden in shadows of massive mesas, is eclipsed by the monumental achievement which crowned a lifetime of selfless labor.

"This isn't just a missionary talking to us in another language—this is God's Word in Navajo. It is just like God talking!" exclaimed one happy reader of the New

Testament. Similar reactions richly rewarded the translator who had been adopted as a member of the Grand Canyon Clan.

Although Faye's friendship was my privilege for many years, she at first resisted any suggestion that her biography be written. It was only on the condition that the story be told "for God's glory alone" that she finally released to me diaries, letters, and personal information which bared the soul of a practical saint humble enough to be mighty in the hand of God.

I would like to express particular appreciation to Faye's Navajo friends who graciously shared with me anecdotes and personal observations, the meat and marrow of Faye's story, as reconstructed by them.

A friend of Navajos, James Fraser of Flagstaff, made available to me valuable ethnological data.

Two non-Navajo friends deserve a special word of thanks: Without the efficient assistance of Wycliffe member Beatrice Meyers the manuscript could not have been ready on the date desired by the publisher. And once again the perceptive editorial assistance of Eleanor Jordan at Harper & Row, who had collaborated on three earlier Wycliffe narratives, made the final phase of the project a pleasure.

ETHEL EMILY WALLIS

Farmington, New Mexico
May 1, 1968

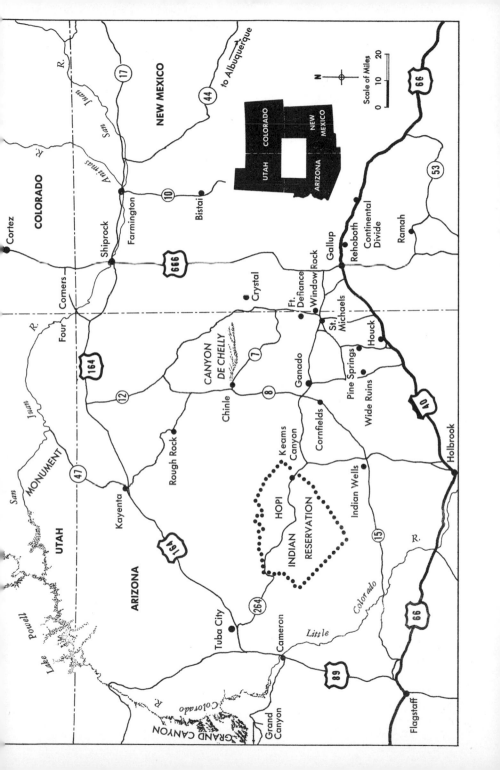

God Speaks Navajo

Prologue

IT WAS late October in northern Arizona. Higher and colder than the rest of the desert state, the pine-clad mountain country was already frostbitten, and the wind had a cutting edge.

Old Navajo men were appraising the wind currents on The Mountain near Flagstaff. These longhairs of the tribe, though illiterate, were skilled in reading the words of the wind and the face of the heavens. They stood erect as the pine trees, their bright red headbands framing leather-brown faces against the deep turquoise sky as they patiently studied the distant clouds.

These prophets and their forefathers had learned the ways of the wind and the clouds and the sky:

Long before Highway 66 invaded their world, cutting a hard, black trail through the heart of the far-reaching dry land where only sheep grazed . . .

Before sports cars and pickups and semitrucks began to whine and whir in a stream of endless motion across the reservation . . .

Before proud jet planes began to spray the blue sky with straight, feathered trails of the white man's clouds . .

The old Indians squinted, and scanned the sky. They turned toward the north and sniffed the wind. Winter would come soon, they said. And it would be a Bad Winter.

As children these practical weather prophets had heard

1

the lore of the winds from their fathers, who had been taught by their grandfathers. They had listened to the chants about the winds, sung perfectly by the older men. One of these songs was called "Windway," and it said:

> Now from somewhere in the skies
> One of the Winds came down to earth;
> And there it happened to be called the Left-handed Wind.

Perhaps this would be the winter of the Left-handed Wind. Or perhaps the spirit of the Sacred Mountain, whose heart is obsidian and whose nerves are kept in motion by the Little Whirlwind, was stirring even now, getting ready for his winter walk.

Whatever they were thinking, they all agreed that there would be a Big Snow. It would come early, before winter was very old, they said.

The old tribal prophets were right. December of 1967 brought a big snow, the biggest in the memory of most living Navajos. Only the very old men had seen such suffering—caused by four feet of snow on the flat desert and twice that much on the slopes. It was a winter of hunger and hardship, of destruction and death. Indians and animals in isolated spots of the reservation perished, buried in snow-smothered hogans.

Many of the younger Navajos had laughed at the men whose knots of black hair were secured at the nape of their necks with bright-colored bands of cloth, old ones who had warned of the bad winter wind laden with heavy white snow.

"Old men's tales," the young ones had said. "We don't believe that stuff anymore."

Modern schools and churches on the reservation had for many years taught that the old ways were only superstitions and were not to be believed. The old ones and their ways had been replaced by new, scientific knowledge. This wisdom, the white men said, was more reliable.

But a Christian woman living at Indian Wells, Arizona, where the 1967 storm was very severe, later confessed, "Had we taken the prediction of the ancient ones among our people seriously, we would have prepared ourselves . . ."

But even now, in the late fall, before the Big Snow, a bone-chilling wind whined down from the peak of Mt. Eldon, called simply The Mountain by the Navajos. The late afternoon sun cast a cool light on the tips of the tall pines which serrated the steep slopes. The wind was gathering strength as it tore at the forest, as if frantically preparing to focus its final fury upon the town at the foot of the mountain. Or perhaps it was just rehearsing for the big snow show, a little more than a month away.

At the base of The Mountain clustered small cottages and cabins, squatting snugly under huge pines, where Indians and white people lived. Inside a one-room cabin a petite white woman sat before a long table which was covered with papers and books. Some of the books lay open, and between them were various piles of papers, handwritten and typed. The table had a cluttered appearance, but as the little woman reached here and there among the piles, first for a book and then for a sheet of paper, it was obvious that she knew their contents by heart. Frail, her hair almost white, she was nevertheless erect and intent, concentrating upon the papers before her.

The woman was Faye Edgerton, who had lived more than half of her seventy-eight years with the Navajo Indians. She was revising the New Testament in the Navajo language, a translation she had finished ten years earlier. It was now in wide use among the people of the largest tribe of the United States. The book had gone through seven printings, and a new edition was needed. Although in delicate health, Faye had determined that the next printing should include a complete revision to make the text more meaningful to Navajo readers. She had found an ideal hideaway near Flagstaff, on the opposite side of the reservation from her home in Farmington, New Mexico, where she had lived and translated for many years.

In contrast to many of the tall Anglo-American missionaries working with the Navajos, Faye was barely five feet tall. Some of the Indians called her the White Woman with Little Feet.

Faye looked up from her work and stopped briefly to listen to the wind, now howling like a coyote in the distance. She shivered and pulled her sweater more tightly around her straight, narrow shoulders. Then she picked up her pen and resolutely continued to write on the paper before her. Her compact hand moved steadily, without hesitation, leaving a trail of bold, well-formed Navajo letters. Writing the Indian language had become almost as natural to her as writing her own native English. For most of her life she had been learning and thinking, teaching and translating, in Diné bizaad, the language of The People, as the Navajos call themselves. Well known to Indians living in the area of Shiprock, the legendary center of the tribe, she was now making new friends on the western side, near Flagstaff.

Delighted with her close Navajo neighbors, Faye would check the revision with them from time to time, in her search for improved renderings of difficult passages. She was especially pleased to find that a group of devout Christians, under the leadership of Mr. Little Man, a Navajo pastor, met for Bible study and worship in a nearby cabin. Their well-worn Navajo New Testaments were signs that they used and loved The Book in their language. Faye visited them occasionally and consulted them about possible changes, to clarify the older text.

She noted that Pastor Little Man and his group were polite, but not eager to assist in changing the words of The Book. However, she continued to ask for suggestions to improve the wording of the Scriptures in Navajo.

Finally one day Pastor Little Man could no longer conceal his disapproval of the white woman's actions. Politely but firmly he challenged her: "What right have *you* to tamper with The Book, God's Word in *our* language?"

Faye straightened herself up to her full five feet and answered, just as firmly: "Well, I translated The Book in your language, and some of *your* people helped me—but it needs to be *improved!* There are places where it does not speak God's Word clearly in the Navajo language!"

Faye's intonation, always emphatic, was very strong. A good friend had remarked: "Once in a while Faye likes a good scrap."

This seemed to be one of those times. But Pastor Little Man was too shocked for combat. He was rocked to the roots by this confrontation, and he could only recover enough spirit to say, "Oh. I did not know that."

Then he said nothing, and his expression did not change. But everything in his silence said: *I'm sorry I spoke, little white woman.*

As they talked, Faye learned that Pastor Little Man's objection was the voice of the group who met in the cabin. Many heated discussions had preceded the decision to register protest, and their leader had been commissioned to speak for them all. There were many questions they wanted to ask:

What is she doing to our Book?

Why is she changing it?

Who gave her permission to do this—or was it just her own thought?

They had no idea that the completion of the New Testament in their language had been Faye's dream for several decades. But their challenge was an honest verbalization of underlying uneasiness on the part of The People who tried to appreciate but could not always understand the attempts of the missionaries to help them. The white man's lack of knowledge of the language, as well as his ignorance of

Indian ways of life, had often hindered mutual cooperation. Very few missionaries had ever attempted to speak the language, so exceedingly hard was it for English tongues and ears. Furthermore, many white people were convinced that Navajo would soon be replaced by English, so why struggle with a difficult language, soon to disappear?

A subtle spirit of religious colonialism, a sort of Christian paternalism, had accompanied the use of English as a dominating language, foreign to Indians. Thus the pattern of much mission work had been characterized by activity on the part of the missionary and passivity on the part of the Indian member of the religious group. Few churches on the reservation were directed, propagated, or supported materially by the Navajo people themselves. To many of them, Christianity was still the white man's religion.

Even the name for God had posed a problem to Navajos. Early missionaries had felt that the native word meaning The-Most-High-Holy-One was heavily freighted with pagan connotation and would not be acceptable as a designation for the Judeo-Christian deity. They insisted upon using the English word "God." But His English name threw up a linguistic barrier for Navajos who sincerely wanted to know this Great Being; even His name was a puzzle. As pronounced by the Indians, "God" sounded much like the Navajo word *gad,* meaning cedar tree. To some, it sounded like *gaagi,* meaning crow. Was this new god, then, a plant or an animal?

When Christmas came and a tall cedar tree was gaily decorated and set up in the front of the church, The People concluded he must be a plant.

Indeed, the first Navajo Christians were hard pressed to unravel the mysteries of the Christian message.

At last, many years later, in 1956, The Book in the language of The People, the Navajo New Testament, was published. It had cost years of persistent dedication to a task and patient perseverance in the face of discouragement. Many individuals had pronounced this translation a pointless project. It would not be used, they had predicted. To these, the grateful reaction of the Navajo people upon the publication of their New Testament had come as a distinct surprise. It enjoyed immediate and enthusiastic acceptance by The People, whose vigorous language was in no danger of disappearing. *God Bizaad,* God's Word, was eagerly embraced by the Navajos as something of value, a treasure in their very own language. This was God's Word spoken expressly to them, not just a book about the white man's God.

Within a few years Pastor Little Man, and hundreds of other Navajos like him, were using The Book, never questioning its origin. Perhaps it had always existed, like God Himself. Or perhaps Little Man had never given a thought as to how The Book came to be. Or perhaps he was like some white men who if pushed might allow that their Book, the King James Bible, had descended from heaven, intact and infallible, let down in a four-cornered sheet.

Whatever Pastor Little Man thought in that moment of truth as he faced the near indignity of his visitor, he was now having quickly to recover his Indian equilibrium.

So this little white woman had written The Book in the language of his people. Unbelievable.

Well, since she had, would she tell The People how their Book came to be?

Then Faye Edgerton told Pastor Little Man of her great desire, for many years, to see God's Word in the language the Navajos could really understand, their own Diné bizaad. And she told how it was finally finished.

It was a long story, too long to tell all at once.

And there were some things that the little woman might never have told Pastor Little Man!

1

Everything's Going My Way!

SHE WAS BORN, appropriately, in 1889, on the eve of the great Gay Nineties. She was born to be happy and loved, carefree and secure. Everything, even the physical setting of her birth, favored Faye Edgerton.

The neat clapboard farmhouse itself seemed to exude an air of serenity. It was planted securely in a protective grove of cottonwood trees on the flat plains of Nebraska. A quiet stream flowed nearby, and on either side as far as the eye could see stretched fertile farmland, productive fields undulating with sturdy stalks of ripening grain. There was nothing in sight, either in the cloudless azure of the prairie sky or on the plush greenness below, to challenge the prosperous appearance of the Midwestern tableau. There was no vestige of the bloody clash of Plains Indians with white settlers, which had stained this very soil only a generation before.

In that encounter the white man had won, and the land for which he fought was now bringing forth a full, painless harvest. It was as if the earth now willingly, effortlessly, produced of itself, bringing unlimited well-being to the white man.

Nor was there sign of the back-breaking struggle or of the free-flowing perspiration that this pleasant sight had cost Gordon Edgerton himself. As a young man he had come from Illinois to homestead the frontier land offered to plucky pioneers. He had gouged out for himself a temporary home in the hills, a dugout in the shallow cliffs of the low-lying hills surrounding Hastings, Nebraska. Then he had worked hard, as hard as any hired hand, from dawn till dark, to tame and groom the land before him. And when it was his, his very own to possess and to plow and to pass on to his children, he built a sturdy little house with the money he had earned by the sweat of his brow.

But the solid little home was not only for himself. It was to be shared with Elva Bird, his bride-to-be, whose family owned a neighboring farm. Slight and slender and scarcely five feet tall, Elva seemed too fragile and feminine for the heavy tasks of a prairie farmwife. But she had come from a durable line of Iowa pioneers, and was accustomed to work.

The Birds had also homesteaded in Nebraska. Elva grew up in a house her father had built, a sod house, constructed of squares of topsoil on which prairie grass grew. Cut out of the earth in uniform pieces, these were building blocks ready to hand for a sound dwelling.

As a young wife, Elva Edgerton worked hard, not only for her own family but also in providing meals for the hired men who worked on the farm. This meant rising early to cook hearty breakfasts and prepare noonday feasts for hungry farmers. Sometimes she had to pack lunch baskets for workers who could not return for the noon meal. One worker, recently from the East and unused to the huge expanses of flatland, would at times insist on taking a lunch with him when he set out in the early morning to plow. It seemed so far to the other end of the field—he was sure he could never make the return furrow by noon!

Gordon and Elva Edgerton were happy homemakers and conscientious parents. Goldie and Arthur, their two older children, were already riding their father's well-fed horses and exulting in the freedom and fun of farm life when their little sister, Faye, appeared on the Nebraska scene. From the day of her birth she was her father's darling. Petite and pretty like her mother, she was winsome, lively, and gay. Large laughing blue eyes dominated a well-formed, squarish doll face. As soon as she could walk, she began to toddle after her father, following him to the barn, chortling and calling in childish adoration. He would turn to see two pudgy baby arms outstretched, rotating in rhythm with gleeful giggles. A headful of dark curls, bouncing and bobbing as if on tiny springs, crowned the small bundle of beauty in motion. She was irresistible—and she knew it.

"I could get *anything* out of my Papa!" she would say, looking back on those magic days of childhood filled only with sunshine. "I was the baby—and I was *spoiled!*"

Petted and pampered and willful, she loved life then, and she lived it fully, with increasing zest, all through the years of her fun-filled youth. Time for serious reflection, and correction of life patterns oriented only to pleasure, could wait until later, much later. Now the days seemed too short for all the happy things to be done.

So scarce were days clouded by unhappiness that when they did come, they made a lasting impression on the sensitive, responsive child. Sorrows which befell her father were especially memorable.

When Faye was still very young, her father moved the family from the farm into the town of Hastings, where he had purchased a grain mill. He was prospering in the business when misfortune struck. One day, without warning, the mill burned to the ground; only a few sacks of grain were salvaged.

"I shall never forget the sight of my dear Papa as he came home after losing the fight with the fire. He was black and charred and exhausted. My mother was wringing her hands and sobbing, 'The mill has burned—the mill has burned.' "

Resourceful and industrious, Gordon Edgerton took the rescued sacks of grain and started a retail feed and grain store. Before long his business was growing and life flowed on once more in unbroken bliss for Faye, his darling and his delight.

So successful was his business that Gordon Edgerton became one of the first citizens of Hastings to own an automobile. And of course his daughter proudly watched as Papa drove the mechanical marvel home for the first time. There was just one small difficulty: Papa could not remember precisely how to *stop* the vehicle! He drove round and round the block, hoping, perhaps, to run out of gas. Finally, in desperation, he simply slowed down, turned resolutely into the driveway, and drove straight inside the garage. A resounding thud against the rear wall settled, for the time being, the problem of how to stop the marvelous new machine.

Cars were scarce in those days, and intersections were relatively uncongested. Faye's father had an original mode of signaling his approach to cross streets. Instead of using the horn he would stick his head out of the window and yell "Hey!" loud and clear. This resounding bellow was effective; any drivers contemplating a crossing stopped dead in their tracks.

Even school held excitement for Faye. Gregarious and sociable, she was always in the center of whatever was going on. Keeping still was an onerous chore, and she was often punished for talking when she should have been doing her sums. The long dark curls, carefully curved and coiled on her mother's finger each morning, seemed to vibrate with vitality. The pretty head would twist and turn, disappear under the heavy oak desk, and then bob up on her neighbor's side. A frequent sight in the lower-grade classroom was that of a tiny girl standing in the corner, her face toward the wall. She looked much like an old-fashioned Valentine, with ruffles at her neck and wrists and at the bottom of a stiffly starched skirt, reaching halfway down a pair of shapely legs.

"You were a naughty girl today—you had to stand in the corner!" her sister Goldie would often scold when they arrived home from school.

"How do *you* know?" Faye would challenge.

"I saw you through a knothole in the floor," was the big sister's convincing answer. The upper-grade classroom was on the second floor, above the lower classes.

"I looked and looked," Faye recalled, "but I never found Goldie's peephole!"

Faye and her family regularly attended the Presbyterian church, where her father was an elder. She attended Sunday School and enjoyed the bright Bible pictures and the cheery songs, for she had a sweet, clear voice and loved to sing. It was not until she was ten years old, however, that the true significance of religion began to impress her. A children's evangelist came to town and held special meetings in the church. When he emphasized waywardness, even in children, and the need for personal forgiveness, she listened well. This was for her. She knew that she should be good, but found it hard to manage. When the evangelist invited the children to kneel and ask God for pardon, Faye quickly responded.

"I was deeply convicted of my own sin and need of a Savior, and when the invitation was given, I was one of the first to go forward."

The early spiritual experience, though sincere, did not seem to effect any vital change in the vivacious girl. She loved sociability wherever she could find it—and it was not always in the church.

"I lived a truly worldly life all through my girlhood," she said later. "My friends were of the same type. The majority of them were from families who were only nominally Christian or who never attended church. My parents deplored my worldly activities but were unable to restrain me. I was very willful and selfish."

2

Our Crowd

"NONE OF OUR CROWD had any strong convictions about anything. We just wanted to have a *good time*." Faye's evaluation of her teen-age friends was accurate. Their goal in life was to enjoy it, and this goal they achieved.

"Our crowd" was composed of half a dozen girls Faye's age, and an equal number of their kind of boys. Their escapades were, in general, typical of adolescent activity in any American town, anytime. But teen-age activities at the turn of the century had a special flavor for fun-loving "Fedgie"—Faye Edgerton, when pronounced rapidly, got shortened into Fedgie, a nickname which stuck all through the glorious turbulence of high school days.

"Here come those darned boys!" was a frequent signal for another battle, feigned or real, with the masculine contingent of the crowd. Without those boys, life would have been exceedingly dull. Pretty and popular, Faye was always on the winning side. Dating and dancing, sleigh riding and skating—or just sitting around with the crowd "doing nothing"—all added up to pure bliss.

Faye's "Dear Diary" was the loyal confidant into whose sympathetic ear she poured her joys and complaints, her

inner struggles and occasional noble aspirations. The entry
for January 1, 1904, seemed to set the pace for "a *very*
good year."

*Jan. 1. At midnight I was out on Steins' front porch giv-
ing three cheers for 1904. Helen had a New Year's party,
and we had a very good time. (I am trying so hard not to
use any slang or bad words and it sounds queer to me to say
"a very good time.") Had fine stuff to eat. (Oh my, just hear
that slang.) New Year's night Duttie came home and some
of us went down to meet her. Then we took her up to
Folletts' and we had a dance . . .*

Helen Stein, a close friend, lived down the street from
Faye, and her home was a rallying center. A gathering of
the crowd frequently ended in a dance, an activity which
Faye loved and in which she excelled. But skating was
fun, too, especially when one was a good skater and popular
with the boys.

*Jan. 5. Went skating on the lake. We skated with our
arms behind us. I like Joe well enough, but when it comes
to skating with him all the time, and "by your leave, Joe,"
when the other kids come up, that's too much!*

Joe's name appeared frequently on the pages of Dear
Diary for several years. But he was not without competition,
for Faye was too full of life to limit the range of her affec-
tions. There were Roy and Will, Harry and Fred, Cecil
and Art—all of the boys were *fun!*

When Faye's parents objected to too many nights out,
there was nearly always a way to manage permission: Papa
could often be persuaded to reverse a decision. He found it
difficult to deny his darling daughter the pleasure she so
deeply desired. The big blue eyes often won their way right
through to Papa's heart and up to his head where decisions
were switched. Faye knew the route well, and she became
a practiced engineer. Her skill once came into play when
a dance date was threatened by a cold. The diary records
the drama:

Sunday. Oh my! I hope this blamed cold is over by Tuesday night. I feel horrid.

Monday. Stayed home all day long. Papa said at noon that I could not go out to the dance, but I didn't say anything and tried my best not to cough.

Tuesday. My cold was lots better and Mamma said at lunch that I could go to the dance if Papa said so. So just before dinner I asked him, and he said "no," that I couldn't go. But I cried and begged and scolded till at last he said I might do as I pleased. Goldie was scolding good-naturedly all the time 'cause Papa didn't stick to his word and make me stay at home, but I doubt if she is so terribly strict with her children when she has them. . . . The floor was simply a dream and we enjoyed ourselves to the utmost. Roy sat next to me going home. After a while I felt something behind me and began to search for the cause and found Roy's arm around me. I made him take it down, but after a little I felt it up there again and all the rest of the way I had to keep making him take it down. Oh! but I was teased about it, and I suppose I'll never hear the last of it, but it wasn't my fault.

Things almost invariably turned out all right for Faye. Sometimes when her family seemed uncooperative, help would come from an unexpected quarter.

Feb. 2. We all went skating in the evening. Papa and Mamma weren't going to let me go. Cecil and Joe came down after me, but Papa said "no" very emphatically and I supposed I was done for. But Mrs. Follett came down in a little while, and she persuaded Papa to let me go.

The Folletts were Faye's good friends and allies. Their home was often a social center or headquarters for planning Campaigns Against the Boys. At one point a boycott of the boys lasted for one long month. The girls were protesting bad behavior by the boys, especially their smoking —and their skating too much at the lake with Grace and Jessie, who were not of "our crowd." Disgusted, Faye's group of girls "ditched the boys" while they were skating with the rivals, and came home with no escorts. Thus began a month-long siege, a delightfully frustrating game of hide-and-seek.

Feb. 9. One week since the new life, as Duttie calls it, began. We girls sat up at Folletts and talked the longest time. Cecil and Joe pay no attention to us, and neither does Art.

Feb. 13. Had oysters at the Chinese restaurant. We are having a fine time while the boys are mad.

Feb. 15. The boys must be getting pretty tired.

For the next three weeks the battle of the sexes went from bad to worse, as the climax of the conflict approached.

Mar. 6. I went up to Folletts. Sangevin and Ella came, and then pretty soon all the boys came traipsing in. They acted so horrid. I wouldn't stay, so I just got up and told Sangevin I was going and then she came and we went to Steins. We fooled around a little while and then came home. Joe and Cecil have the most cheek of anybody I know. Joe hasn't any will of his own, either. When Cecil is around he won't speak to any of us (we don't speak to him unless he speaks first) and then when Cecil is gone, he is so sweet and nice.

Rapport with the boys deteriorated until things looked hopeless indeed. For consolation one night the girls had a slumber party. Sometime during the slumberless evening "the hall doors opened and there stood four tramps with the faces of Joe and Fred and Johnny and Art. We all laughed, and then everything was all right."

Morality crusades to reform the boys were notably short-lived, but the diary is sprinkled with traces of these sporadic efforts, such as: *Agnes got to talking about how the boys acted and the girls immediately formed a club, the chief object of which is to make the boys act decent. We are never going to let the boys smoke in our presence, but we're not going to be high and mighty about it. We're just going to be nice.*

Games for outguessing Papa and outwitting the boys furnished plenty of zest and just plain entertainment for the gay young girl who was always hungry for something to happen. Struggles involving her mother and conflicts with conscience were more serious. She shared with her diary the pangs of regret which pained her one day when she had broken a promise to her mother. She had gone to a friend's house and stayed long beyond time to return home. *I stayed till Mamma came after me. She talked to me so on the way home, that I think I'll keep my promises after this, if I break my neck to do it. Dear Mamma, she loves me so and feels so bad when I don't do right. I just hate it, but still I act this way. I think there must be something the matter with me, for no other girl would do it, I know.*

On rare occasions Faye's better self would get the upper hand, and an entry would indicate the joy of a good conscience: *To please Mamma, I went to church in the evening. All the kids went down to Marguerite's and danced till after ten—but I was glad I went to church anyway.*

More typical of entries concerning church were such notes as: *Went to church and Sunday School as usual. Dr. Elliott preached and I thought he would never get through.*

Church seemed to give Faye enough religion to make her uncomfortable, but not enough to help permanently in the upward struggle. She was impressed on one occasion when the preacher: *talked about Daniel, and his theme was* do right, *always and forever do right, regardless of the conse-quences*—don't compromise.

But within a few days the diary betrayed a smarting de-feat:

Tuesday night. I went to a pre-Lent dance with Biddy. I knew all the time I ought not to go, but I wasn't strong enough not to. I think I will be the next time, though, when

*I know I ought not to go. Didn't have such an awfully good
time for that very reason. Went to church first to ease my
conscience, but it didn't help any. It bothered me just as
much.*

Even visits to churches outside the Presbyterian pale did
not fill the spiritual vacuum which at times haunted her:

*Sunday. I went to the Catholic church this morning and
I must say I wouldn't like to belong to it unless I was the
priest, which I couldn't very well be. But the altar was pretty
with all its candles.*

Faye's days were mostly lived on high plateaus of pure
pleasure, interrupted only briefly now and then by a gully
of gloom. More often than not she would summarize the
week's activities with such words as: *This has been a fine
week. I've had an awfully good time and I'd like to have it
all over again! I feel so good tonight I could do almost anything!"*

Although pleasure was first in Faye's book, she was a good
student and somehow managed to stay at the top of her
class. But studies were never allowed to interfere with those
delightful gatherings of her crowd. She seemed to be con-
fident of success in both departments, as the diary would
often reveal: *Algebra and rhetoric finals tomorrow. I hope
I have exemption grades. I know I will in algebra, but
rhetoric—oh, well, I don't care. I'll get along all right anyway.*

Another time she wrote: *Friday. Latin exam, but I was
exempt, thank goodness. We went out to Rittenhouse's grove
to get wood specimens for botany. We went from one end
to the other of that big grove and only got about 5 specimens
when we might have had 50. But we were out for a good
time. We made a fire in the road and baked some apples
Duttie took along. Sangevin said hers was all the better for
the half inch of dirt on it. Mine was fine, so nice and juicy.*

Every school has its kill-joys. There is evidence that one
of the teachers had it in for Faye and company: *Got called*

*up for a lecture on the cat yells we gave when we passed the
school Friday afternoon. Someone happened to see us wave
to Hugh as we passed and that was the cause of it all. . . .
Just because Helen and I whisper a little we are kept in
almost every other night.*

More serious, however, was the time Faye fibbed. It all
happened after a big basketball game, Hastings against
South Omaha, when she and a friend cut school to go to
the train to say good-bye to the boys of the visiting team:

*Tues. Hazel and I sneaked out and went down to the
train. Then I came home and she went to school. Tonight
Steime and I were called in and asked us if we were absent
without permission. Steime wasn't of course, but I was, and
then I told a big story about a headache etc., but was
finally cornered and forced to tell the truth, I'm sorry to say.
I never felt so cheap in all my life, and tomorrow I'm going
to tell the whole truth and take the consequences.*

*Wed. Well, here I am delaying, putting off as usual—
really, I get so mad at myself but when it comes right down
to doing it, somehow I can't. I will tomorrow or die, and
nothing shall hinder me.*

*Thurs. Well, I did it, today after school. It took an awful
lot of nerve but mercy, how happy I was afterward! Felt like
a new person.*

High school days ended in a full burst of glory, with an
exhausting round of class activities. In the class play, *Just
Out of College,* Faye starred with much success. A full social
calendar, with a wardrobe of new clothes for every occasion,
was the fulfillment of all her fond dreams. Some of the joys
were shared with the diary:

*Apr. 9. Went to the Elks' dance in the evening with Fred.
Had the loveliest time! Danced 4 times with Adam. I hate
him—or almost do—and he always asks me. Wore my new
pumps that I got Thurs. They are beauties! Had the best
kind of a time.*

May 12. The banquet wasn't a bit formal. When the fel-

lows played Turkey in the Straw, everyone pounded the tables with their spoons and kept time with their feet. Went with Roy and had the best time. Danced half the time with Roy, but I rather liked that for he's such a dandy dancer.

Our commencement was the grandest success. Our play was the biggest hit ever. Everyone said that it was the best amateur play ever given here—ahem!

During the year after high school Faye's life was filled with the study of music and dates with Harry. She studied both piano and organ, and began to give piano lessons. It soon became apparent that Harry held less fascination for Faye than her music.

Jan. 28. Refused Harry tonight and went up to St. John's by myself just for the walk. Harry almost took it for granted that he might walk home with me tonight. It's good for him not to think so.

Feb. 15. Yesterday was Valentine's Day and I got a bunch of white sweet peas from Harry—awfully pretty and so fragrant. Last night we went to the Y. P. Society party. Had an awfully good time, only Harry provoked me by some of the foolish things he wrote in my "wish-book." It's the very first time he ever did anything like that. I do hope he doesn't keep it up. I simply ignored it. It was nice of him to send the flowers, though.

Mar. 5. I turned Harry down tonight. I should think he'd stop asking me every night, but he doesn't! I suppose I'd feel hurt if he didn't though.

Mar. 21. Asked to be organist at St. Marks. Choir leader asked Harry to sing in the choir, which I don't like. Everywhere I go, there is Harry. Guess I'll have to stop somewhere, both this narrative and my going with Harry.

Faye was making a decision about Harry. There was no future in going with him for the sake of having an escort, and she quite abruptly terminated the twosome. She had been thinking about the direction her life would take, so she made a decision, turning a sharp corner. And she left a somewhat puzzled Harry standing there, scratching his head.

3

Too Frivolous for a Missionary

BY BRACING herself on the edge of the organ bench and stretching her short legs their full length, Faye managed to manipulate the three-consoled organ in the Presbyterian church. John Rees, her capable instructor, had coached his undersized but capable pupil to a high point of proficiency, and she became the church organist.

Under the further tutelage of another instructor, she had also become an efficient piano teacher, with the following recommendation: "I consider Miss Faye Edgerton a very capable pianist, and during her several years of study with me I have always found her to be a conscientious and thorough student. Aside from her musical ability I think that she possesses the requisites for a good instructor of music, and to those desiring such I gladly recommend her."

In addition to teaching music, Faye was her father's business assistant, and of course the partnership was most compatible. Music, however, became a dominating interest, and she decided to make it a career. Her sister, Goldie, was now married and living in Chicago, where good musical training was available. For two years Faye lived with Goldie and her husband, studying music and enjoying the cultural advantages of the big city. The two happy years passed very quickly.

Upon returning to Hastings, Faye soon had a growing clientele of piano pupils. A music class in a town an hour away by train took Faye once a week from the busy routine in her home town. It was during this busy teaching schedule that she became gravely ill with scarlet fever. Her life was in danger for several weeks, and she almost completely lost her hearing. There were days of deep concern for her parents, and weeks of recovery when she was practically isolated in a world of silence.

This illness was a time of crisis in Faye's life. She had been very actively involved in church work, but a personal knowledge of God was lacking. There had been a vacuum in her life, and now she had time to think seriously. The frivolity of adolescence had given place to happy usefulness as a music teacher, but her life seemed to be without purpose. She was not really happy. Now the threat of total and permanent deafness forced her to face issues more seriously than she ever had before. Up until now there had been no big problems; everything had gone her way.

One day, very suddenly, in a burst of wonderful sound, her hearing returned! Faye was deeply grateful, for she realized that God Himself had spared her life and now had restored her power to hear. She would never be the same again; the presence of God was now a joyous reality.

When she was strong once again she began to realize that her mother and father had been working hard and had been under a long strain. They needed a long vacation, something they had never had. She made that rest possible.

"For one whole summer my father's helper, 'Pat the Irishman,' and I ran the business. I really enjoyed that!" Faye reminisced. The responsibility of managing a commercial business was for her a stimulating experience.

"But I felt that my life wasn't counting for very much," she continued. "Although I was very active in church and young people's work, a sense of purpose was missing."

During the following fall an innovation in the church

program held part of the answer for Faye. A team of evangelists from the Moody Bible Institute were invited to hold meetings, something which had never before happened in the Presbyterian church of Hastings. The messages given were dynamic, Bible-centered, and eye-opening for her. And the music was excellent! Faye greatly admired the pianist and struck up a friendship with her. She urged Faye to consider attending Moody. This appealed to the ambitious young woman who now was ready to devote her life to God's service.

When Faye told her parents that she was considering training for Christian service, her father said, "Well, if that's what you want, go ahead." But there was understandable disappointment. He had hoped for a permanent business partner who would eventually take over completely.

The first days of study at Moody were days of heaven on earth for Faye, for she learned much about the Bible which she had never heard before. The belief in a future bodily return of Christ to the earth was a new teaching for her. This, related to the missionary task of taking the gospel to people in faraway lands who had never heard it, was a revelation. The direction of her life was quickly shifting; she would never be the same again.

Suddenly, in the midst of such stimulating studies, her mother sent word that Faye's father was seriously ill and unable to carry on the business. It was necessary for his daughter to leave the school which she already loved and return to help care for her father and for his business.

As her father slowly recovered, he said to Faye one day, "If you want the business, I'll give it to you."

"No, Papa," she quickly answered. "I don't want it. I am going into Christian work."

The following spring the business was sold, and Faye returned to Moody. During the following two years while she finished her course she made a decision: she would give her life to Christ for foreign mission service.

When a close friend in Hastings heard the news she said, "Faye is the *last* person I thought would be a missionary— she's so frivolous!"

But the friend did not know the new Faye. She had many friends in Chicago—those whom she met when she had studied music and new friends now from her Moody association—but the old frivolity was gone; the joy of solid purpose replaced it.

When Faye wrote home that she was being considered by the Presbyterian mission board for work in Korea, her mother was shocked. Although Mrs. Edgerton had worked diligently in the women's missionary society in Hastings, she had never dreamed that her daughter would actually think of going so far from home to propagate the gospel. She wrote in a tearstained letter: "It's all right with me if you go, for I feel I can't hold you back, but it's going to be hard . . ."

4

Korean Crisis

SEATTLE WAS AGLOW with the golden reflection of sunset cast upon her clean face from the smooth surface of the Pacific. The port city bade a noncommittal farewell to the small Japanese vessel moving reluctantly from her shore. The ship appeared dwarfed, and quite defenseless, against the endless ocean which gradually engulfed it. But the ominous expanse of water itself was soon devoured by the descending darkness.

Faye watched the city sink from sight. She finally found

relief from the pent-up pain of parting in the friendly shadows of the ship's deck, where she could sob in silence. She had held up bravely as she kissed her mother good-bye and turned quickly for the final walk up the gangplank. She had even fought off the desire to cry while waving as long as she could discern the figure of her little mother, waving bravely in return.

In the fall of 1918 Mrs. Edgerton had accompanied Faye to New York, where together they had enjoyed the sights of the big city and the company of Presbyterian mission personnel. Now it had come, that dreaded departure, and it was *hard,* just as her mother had predicted. Roots driven deep into Nebraska soil and the intertwined fiber of family affection felt the pull. A fond father back at home in Hastings was sharing the pangs of separation in lonely silence. The house that had once resounded with girlish giggles and merry music was quiet, too quiet.

Faye could hardly believe that she was really on her way to a new land and a new life. As all that was dear and familiar irrevocably receded, a strange nostalgia settled upon her. But the companionship of Mr. and Mrs. Edwin Campbell, missionaries returning to Korea after their first furlough, softened the separation from her homeland. She was soon absorbed in learning the Korean alphabet, which the Campbells offered to teach her. All the way across the Pacific she diligently studied the script and syllables of the strange new language. When she arrived in Korea she was able to read quite fluently, even before beginning formal study of the language. She was determined to lose no time in preparing herself for her new life.

After several weeks of alternate gliding and chopping over the ocean the Japanese ship had finally made its way through the Yellow Sea, around the coast of China, and up to the craggy shoreline of Korea. Dozens of tiny jagged islands jutted up abruptly from the intensely blue water.

As the missionary party disembarked and then rode in an open taxi from the port up the narrow, winding road to Seoul, Faye knew that she had indeed been transported to another world. The contrast between the prairie flatness where she had lived and the rugged mountains of the land which was to be home could not have been more dramatic. She was now in a peninsular outjutting of rocks and rivers, surrounded by stormy seas. It was a land of narrow, crowded streets and steeply terraced hills. Pagodas and Buddhist temples were a far cry from the square, calm lines of Midwestern churches. Mulberry trees and huge conical heaps of silkworm hives were exotic sights to thrill a newcomer from America.

During her first weeks in Korea, intensive periods of language study were relieved by occasional sight-seeing trips or expeditions into rural areas. Her old practice of sharing joys with her journal was continued in her new home. But now the entries had a different flavor. Almost every notation was concluded with a spontaneous word of doxology, or a self-directed sermonette. On one of her first trips out of the city she wrote: *Yesterday went to see Nine Dragon Falls— such rugged and majestic scenery I've never seen before! The awe of God grows in one's heart as one beholds such beauty. Yet that God is* my *heavenly Father!*

On another occasion, a verbal vignette depicted rural beauty in early morning: *Saw the sunrise, and the vision of the valley with its yellow barley fields, rice fields, and plowed ground, with lavender and blue mountains in the background. It was a vision of Korea: partly sown, partly plowed, partly ready for harvest—but* all *waiting for workers.*

Faye's first winter was spent out in the country mission station of Chunju where she worked intensely studying the language. There were continual opportunities for speaking Korean with the charming children, clothed in padded garments, who played in the congested village streets. And there was always conversation with the simple country folk who attended the services, held in quaint little chapels. Faye marveled at the devotion of these Christians who even in bitter cold weather came in great numbers to early morning prayer meetings.

Even during her first winter in Korea the effects of the severe weather were evident as her health began to suffer. The little charcoal burners over which she huddled to study furnished only symbolic protection from the cruel cold. Trips through the snow against bitter winds to visit outlying chapels soon began to inflict permanent damage. Severe sinusitis which was to plague her for the rest of her life developed rapidly. Although it sapped her strength, she tried to ignore it and worked long hours in order to pass her language examinations. She did well in the language and was able to teach women's classes in the village chapels.

The following spring a new strain was added to further tax the new missionary. On March 1, 1919, the brutal struggle between Korea and Japan began with the cry of independence: *Mansei!* Long live Korea! The Korean Christians with whom Faye was closely associated were the special targets of Japanese wrath. Accused of insurrection and rebellion, some of them were beaten, others burned to death. Terror and violence in open evidence everywhere were a shock to Faye's sensitive nerves. Her diary entries reflect turmoil, political and personal:

March 1. Uprisings in Seoul, Pyeng Yang, and Syen Chun. Declaration of Independence signed by 33 representative Koreans sent to the Governor General—no violence used. All the men were arrested and are now in jail; many prominent pastors among them.

March 3. Funeral for Prince Yi, last emperor of Korea. More disturbances throughout Korea.

April 20. Easter Sunday. Police searched our house for one of the leaders—went into every room except the one he was in!

May 6. Felt dizzy and depressed today. People say it is the weather. Nearly fell down on the street.

Erosion of health, now compounded by emotional strain, threatened a stability already tested by the adjustments involved in living in a strange new world. Try as she would, Faye could not fight off the desire to give up and return home.

Once in an hour of black despondency she asked a senior missionary to loan her enough money for a ticket back to America. The wise colleague, sympathetic but firm, refused, saying, "All new missionaries get discouraged. Just stick it out for a while, and you'll be all right."

"Sticking it out" was tough business for one who each day had to struggle for energy to live. Nothing was easy in Korea. In a letter written after her first hard year she said:

I have felt like a little child who was just beginning school, since I left my inland home on the prairies of Nebraska to make the long journey across mountains and sea to this strange, unknown land. Every day, from the time I left home, I've learned something—and it hasn't all been Korean, either!

It has been a real privilege to meet and know the Korean Christians. Their courage, their endurance, their supreme faith in the God of the helpless in this, their hour of trial, is an inspiration indeed.

Slowly Faye recovered from a first hard year, which had been climaxed by a nervous breakdown that seemed to spell a premature end to her first term of service. Although she never fully regained the physical strength she had lost, she was able to continue her work. A time of rest and renewal at the resort of Wonsan, where experienced and spiritual missionaries prayed with her and helped her back to a life of usefulness, was never forgotten. During days of recovery she often mentioned the name of fellow worker, Gerda Bergman, in her diary. Gerda had been a strong arm to comfort and admonish one to whom deep trouble was a stranger. Loving and helpful, Gerda was also evidently quite frank. Once Faye wrote: *Gerda spoke to me today, and the Lord Himself seemed to be speaking through her, telling me the lessons I should learn from that experience:* self-control *and* self-effacement *in all things; that Faye Edgerton must be seen and not heard; that Jesus must be seen in me.*

On Thanksgiving Day, 1920, Faye again referred to the help of Gerda's friendship:

The greatest blessing this year has been the experience of coming to know Christ better, an abiding consciousness of His presence. Bound up with this experience is the friendship of Gerda Bergman through whom God brought me to this blessed place, the true land of Canaan.

Gerda was a stalwart woman, strong in body and spirit. She was a hard worker, loved by missionaries and Koreans, whose language she spoke like one of them. Born in Sweden in 1886, she came to America in 1892 and grew up in the state of Washington. She went to Korea in 1915 and very soon was placed in positions requiring knowledge of the language and mature powers of judgment. Her physical and spiritual vitality seemed endless. Long years of future service were to prove Gerda's inner strength. She was to work continuously in Korea until World War II, when she would be taken prisoner by the Japanese. Interned for thirty-one months, she would nearly die of malnutrition. Finally rescued and returned to the States in 1945, she was to return to Korea two years later. In 1950 she would again be tested by war, and evacuated to Japan, where she would carry on work with Korean refugees. She was to return to America for well-earned retirement only to find that she could not stay away from Korea, and in 1957 she would return to the land which was truly home. Not until 1967 would she consent to return to the States to stay.

This was Gerda, loving friend and strong counselor, who helped Faye in her hour of deepest need.

By the end of 1920 Faye was able to go to Syen Chun, her permanent place of service during the following years in Korea. Of that move she wrote home: "After stopping in three places to gather my scattered belongings I arrived at last in Syen Chun, and it surely was good to feel that at last the time had really come when I could unpack and stay put!"

She taught women's classes in the Bible institute. One time, while teaching First and Second Corinthians, she wrote to a friend: "I went down into the valley of discouragement as I struggled in limited Korean to adequately expound the wonderful chapter on love and the one on the resurrection."

In spite of the struggles, the experience was joyful. She wrote: "It was an inspiration to see all those 1,050 women who had given up a whole week to study the Bible. Some of them had walked all the way from Changsung, a three days' trip."

The sacrificial giving of poor women impressed Faye. If they had no money they gave salable articles such as jewelry, clothing, and switches of hair.

In Kuchin, where a church building was needed, the young girls gave their precious wedding clothes and their jewelry. The deep sincerity of Korean Christians and the responsibility they took for extending the gospel were an eye opener to Faye.

It was during this phase of service in Korea that she discovered the secret of the strength of the Korean church. This discovery formed a principle which would guide her labor in later years. The Korean people studied firsthand a Bible well translated into their own language; it was printed in the "people's alphabet," a simplified phonetic orthography which even uneducated peasants could learn to read quickly and well. Devised centuries earlier, it had not been widely used until Protestant missionaries arrived the latter part of the nineteenth century. The difficult Chinese character script was until then the recognized medium for written communication in the Korean language.

When the first Presbyterian missionaries began work in Korea they found the educated class reading literature written in Chinese characters. Only a small minority of the people could read and write; the country was practically illiterate. When the translation of the Korean Bible was completed, the missionaries risked the wrath of the educated class and began publishing literature in the despised *eunmun*, which was so simple that "even a woman could learn it." It had been devised by the good King Sejong in 1446, with the help of a committee of scholars. But its simplicity had been spurned by the literate few.

Although the use of the simplified alphabet alienated the educated class for a time, it became "an instrument of incalculable value in making the Christian movement general among the people," as reported in the early annals of the Presbyterian mission. Widespread Bible reading in this script, coupled with the "indigenous" church principle, made the Korean church "self-propagating, self-governing, and self-supporting." It produced a healthy national church body, free from the "rice" Christianity which had characterized early mission work in China.

"At once nearly all the Korean Christians were literate," said an early report. "Suddenly a people who sat in darkness saw the great light—through the printed page." Korea suddenly became more literate than any of the surrounding countries of Asia, most of which were "character"-using cultures.

It was this literate, vigorous community of Korean Christians which made a lasting impact upon Faye's spirit. As she sat with humble people, teaching them to read the Bible or to sing from the hymnal in their mother tongue, she felt the force of primitive homegrown Christianity in native soil. The faith of these folk would not be easily shaken; the foundation was their own, not a foreign importation.

Although now adjusted in mind and spirit, Faye showed little physical improvement. By the end of 1922 it seemed wise that she return to America for the treatment of a worsening sinus condition.

Leaving Korea was a painful experience. Faye loved the Korean people and their language, which she had labored to learn well. She had grown to love the wild beauty of the rugged little mountain country, and she loved her work.

The sadness of leaving was accentuated by the knowledge that with undermined health she might never return. Her sharp disappointment was offset only by the desire to see her beloved father, who had been recently confined to bed and whose health was failing rapidly.

A brief entry written with restrained emotion concluded a full, bitter-sweet chapter spanning four eventful years:

Nov. 19. Arrived home. Papa sits up some in the morning and in the afternoon. He said when he saw me, "She looks just as natural!"

5

Navajo Initiation

WITH THE PEACEFUL death of her father in December, 1923, one full act of Faye's life, composed of many varied scenes, was concluded. The next year the curtain rose in a land worlds away, though geographically not far from Nebraska.

The Presbyterian board in 1924 assigned Faye to work on the Navajo reservation in Arizona, in a climate which might, it was thought, help her sinus condition. Her generally weakened physical condition also made it advisable that she be near medical aid. Faye arrived at the Ganado mission in the spring of the year, when the desert was dressed in its Sunday best. Out in the dry land, dedicated pioneers had built a self-contained mission town, a church-school center for Indian children to whom white ways were completely foreign. Located sixty miles from the railroad in Gallup, it was in the heart of sun-baked Navajoland.

The mission received its water from a government reservoir a few miles away. It mined its own coal from the surrounding mountains, which were also its source for lumber. The dry arroyos provided building material for adobe brick, lime, and calcimine. Older Indian boys had helped in the construction of the impressive complex, a whole community of big buildings, alone in the desert, where 150 Indian children were being educated.

The trip from Nebraska to Gallup, and then to Ganado, was filled with exotic sights for the new worker. Although Faye had traveled in the Orient, she was impressed by this wonderful new world nearer home.

Describing her train trip, she wrote to her mother:

We had to wait several hours in Denver, and then passed over the mountains in the night. The scenery was pretty and mountainous in the morning until we came to Albuquerque. We stopped there thirty minutes. There is a beautiful hotel, built of stucco, Spanish style, surrounded by several courts with green grass, flowers, and fountains. At the station there are several Indian curio rooms. One was a Navajo room where women and girls were weaving rugs and spinning the woolen yarn, and with them were some cute little papooses. Outside Indian women and men were selling pottery and bows and arrows. There were so many things to see, and we had just begun when we heard "All aboard" and had to leave. From there on it was mostly sagebrush and sand and rock. Every once in a while there was a little town with houses made of adobe brick.

We were met at Gallup by Mr. Fred Mitchell, the supervisor of the Ganado mission, and started on our 6o-mile ride to Ganado. We crossed over two mountain ridges, both of which are much higher than Ganado which is about 6,500 feet. The ridges were covered with pine, cedar, and pinyon trees and were very pretty. The low flat places between the mountains are covered with sagebrush and very short grass. Everything looked better than I expected. The only houses we passed on the way were Indian trading stores about every ten miles.

It was toward evening when we arrived. When we were within about a mile of Ganado we could see the electric lights and it seemed quite like civilization to see nice and orderly buildings around the campus, a dozen or so of them.

Faye was impressed with the Indian girls in gingham dresses, "their black hair combed neatly and tied with big bows." Very soon she was in a full swing of activities with them, helping in the dormitory and in the classes. Her ability in music was most helpful for teaching the children to sing and play the piano.

The older boys went to school half days; the rest of their time was spent in work on the campus. There were a bakery, a laundry, a powerhouse, and a carpenter shop where much manual labor was done. Some of the older boys and girls, she noted, were studying the Bible to become Christian workers among their own people. This training was all in English, and Faye reported, they "are not allowed to talk Navajo, except after supper." Speaking in their own mother tongue was something like a special dessert, reserved for a few delicious moments at the close of the day.

The mission leaders were following the philosophy of education of the Indians that was then in vogue: the best

way to train young tribesmen is to encourage them to forget
the hogan and all that it represents. Suppression of the use
of the Indian language was standard procedure in government and mission schools. Indian children were made to feel
that speaking in their mother language did not represent
progress; it was part of the old way, which must be forgotten.

The year 1924 was in a decade of transition in Navajo
history. The humiliating corralling at Fort Sumner under
the surveillance of Kit Carson was long past but not forgotten
by the older Indian leaders. The Navajo people had been
decimated, but not defeated, by white men who later confessed that they had without reason wronged a whole nation.
In 1868, when the tribe had been released from their desert
jail, a battered handful of survivors, a mere four thousand,
had led their few sheep back to the dry land and started all
over again. They had had but two sharp arrows in their
quiver: their language, their very own Diné bizaad; and an
indestructible corollary, the Navajo will to live as a nation.
With these they would win.

Life under the high hand of the white rulers was hard.
Government representatives on the reservation, though often
honestly desiring to aid the Indian in building a new life,
were misguided. There was a constant watch to keep the
young people from "going back to the blanket," to sever
them from Navajo family life. Patterns of living centered in
the clan system of the matriarchal society were labeled Bad.
Students who backslid to the ways of the hogan were educational fatalities, cultural failures.

Yes, 1924 was in a decade before trained linguists would
accord the Navajo language its place in the academy of
adequate forms of human communication; before such linguists as Edward Sapir and Harry Hoijer would analyze its
complicated grammatical structure; and two decades before
anthropologists such as Clyde Kluckhohn would guide edu-

36 GOD SPEAKS NAVAJO

cators toward using the Indian language and culture as allies in the process of preparing tribespeople to take their place in American society.

In the twenties, the clash of Indian mores with the white man's ways was often cruel. Young Indians were habitually humiliated by uneducated bureaucrats who had no respect for basic human dignity and regarded tribesmen as less than worthy of sympathetic treatment in institutions under their supervision. Teachers in Indian schools were often guilty of mental, if not physical, cruelty to their students. These children would often escape and run for the shelter of the hogan where they were loved and secure—never mind the scant rations and sheep watching! The runaways were sometimes rounded up like cattle, loaded into trucks, and forcibly taken back to jail-like boarding schools. Oliver La Farge, in his perceptive portrayal of the underlying integrity of the Navajo people, even under duress at the hand of small-minded white men, dramatizes the facts in his novel *The Enemy Gods*. He depicts a wise old Indian counseling a young son who rebels at the humiliation suffered at school. The old man says to the lad:

"No, my grandson. You want this schooling, even if it is hard. There are many tribes of Long-Haired People, of Earth People, many strong warriors, but this one tribe, the *Bellacana*, conquered them all. Why? Because he knows more, I think. By paper and by wires he talks to his friends in the distance, he leaves his words behind him when he goes away. He makes things we cannot make. He is here, he is all around us, we cannot get rid of him. Therefore we must learn his secrets that we, Navajos, may continue. Long ago we asked for these schools. We want them. It is not pleasant for you, but you need it, I think."

To another young Indian who is being shamed into denying his identity with his own race, he says:

"Now you, grandchild, I think you are making a mistake, too. If you learn all the white man's way and forget the Navajo, if that happens to our young men, then we die, we are destroyed, as surely as if by warfare. The man who will serve his people in the years to come, the man who will strengthen them is the man who can learn all of the one without losing the other. That is what we are hoping for, we who used to be warriors and leaders, and who still wear the old-fashioned clothes." *

There were advantages, obvious advantages, in talking to friends in the distance "by paper and by wires." It was good for a man to "leave his words" in permanent form, even when he went away. But all of these good things came in a white package; there was little on paper in the Navajo language. Legends and myths captured in written form were only for museums and libraries.

Even mission schools shared the mentality of the times, which led to the prohibition of the use of the mother tongue and the exaltation of the white man's language. Christianity and progress were often equated with embracing Anglo-American dress and speech. This superficial brand of conversion often resulted in disillusionment and disappointment for the missionary and frustration for the Indian.

Notable exceptions to such failure are preserved in the words of some of the first pupils in mission schools where the love of Christ shone through the efforts of dedicated teachers. And although the Navajo language was considered too difficult for practical use, some few missionaries had made attempts to learn it and had translated portions of the Bible into it. The early Catholic missionaries at the St. Michaels mission had made efforts to reduce the language to a practical written form.

At Tolcheco, a small outstation about forty miles from

* Popular Library Edition (New York, 1965), p. 37.

Ganado, Mr. Mitchell had supervised a school and had taught a small group of Indian children. Some of these had learned to read and to write in their own language. One older boy had gone back to his hogan at vacation time and excited his fourteen-year-old brother about going to school. He had taught him to write in the Navajo language. The young brother wrote a letter in Navajo, requesting permission to enter the Tolcheco school. It was dated the Month of the Crusted Snow (December) 25, 1919, and the English translation read: "At Tolcheco, they say, you are starting the school again. I want to go there. I wish to be a pupil to learn God's Word. Because I am going to learn to read God's Word I am very happy. I am very happy thinking about it. I must be a pupil. That is all I am thinking about. Tell me about the school."

The letter was signed by Billy Gorman, who attended the school and later became an educated and influential member of the Navajo Council.

Quite often a young Indian would make a choice between two less than ideal situations: an unhappy home life where there was family trouble and a school under rigid foreign regime. The story of Hard-Arrow-Wood, a young fellow in school at Ganado during Faye's early years on the staff, is quite typical of those who received positive benefits from missionary efforts:

I am a full-blooded Indian, born in the heart of Navajo country east of Indian Wells and about forty miles north of where the Santa Fe Railway now runs through Holbrook, Arizona.

I am the eldest of six brothers and my father's name is The-Man-Who-Has-Cattle. He left us when we were still too young to take care of ourselves. He is still living but has another family.

In my boyhood I worked for my uncle just like a
slave. His word was like an iron rod. Many a time before daylight I was awakened by his whip and driven
out of the hogan and into the ice-river or into the
snow to roll in it naked so that I would be hardened
to the cold.

When I was seventeen years old I ran away from my
uncle because he whipped me so hard. I went back to
my mother who was working hard to take care of my
brothers and sisters. I helped her with the sheep.

One of my brothers went away to school and came
back with a view of life different from what we had. He
became interpreter for the first missionary who came
to our part of Navajo country at Ganado. He was the
first one that told me about Jesus the Savior of men.
At first I did not understand. But this little seed of
truth which I received from the first missionary slowly
sprang up in my heart. It grew, because it was the seed
of God's Word.

Other young men like Hard-Arrow-Wood became Faye's
friends. She loved them from the day she first saw them
working and laughing and learning at the mission school.
She even tried to learn some words of their intriguing language, but it was difficult to pronounce, and there were no
lesson books available. Besides, English was the *lingua franca*
in the school, and there was no real need to learn the Indian
tongue. Faye thought, however, that speaking their language
would help in getting close to the youngsters, would help
in understanding and solving their problems. But she complied with the rules of the mission and accepted an interpreter, a bilingual Indian girl who could communicate with
Navajos for her. This "mouth of the missionary" would accompany Faye to hogans in the desert surrounding the school,

where she would visit and teach the Indian people about
Christ.

Faye's interpreter during her first year at Ganado was
Grace Segar, an intelligent Navajo girl who was a jolly companion and a capable go-between for her own people. During
their days of travel together over the desert, Faye asked her
many questions and heard how she came to Ganado. She had
first attended Mr. Mitchell's school in Tolcheco, which she
had entered as a very small, scared Indian child. After many
adventures, in and out of school, she came back to work at
Ganado. She told of her early days:

I entered school when I was small; I was only about
seven years old. I came to school not knowing a word
of English. I didn't know a spoon from a fork or a fork
from a spoon. Before I came to school they used to
scare us, and tell us that great big creatures with aprons
would come and steal us and run off with us. In those
days the white women used to wear big aprons, big
enough to hide a child in. When I first came to school
I kept watching one white woman who wore a big
apron. Then I was taken into the presence of the super-
intendent, a man with a great big black moustache. He
looked at me. I was trembling in my moccasins with
my little old blanket wrapped around me. I didn't
know what was going to happen.

He smiled and said to me in Navajo, "Come to me,
my child." In that moment all my fear went away. I
went over there and he put his arms around me. Then
he handed me over to one of those creatures with a big
apron.

I was in school for several years. Then one day after
I had been home for vacation I decided that I would
rather stay home. I would like to learn the ways of my
people. I wanted to learn to weave and to make food

out of cornmeal. So I stayed home and learned how to put cornmeal in the corn husk and bake it in the ashes.

At first I enjoyed it, but we were poor and we didn't have much to eat. We didn't have a wagon, so I carried all the wood and the water on my back. I herded sheep. I learned to card and spin wool, and I learned to weave. I stayed there in my home for eighteen months, and I learned many things. Those eighteen months were almost a lifetime. But there was a gnawing in my heart which said: *What are you doing here?*

Then my folks started to talk about giving me away to some medicine man so that he could bring in the earnings. My mother, who had been married very young, kind of protected me. But the rest of my relatives gathered and said that I should have a home of my own, that I was getting to be an old lady. I was only fifteen or sixteen, but it got pretty serious. My mother had been protecting me, but then she also began to think that I should marry this man.

That scared me, so I went up on the top of the mesa where I could see clear over into the next valley, over by Navajo Mountain. I just sat there, and the thought came to me: *What are you doing here? You're not helping your people any. You haven't even nerve enough to convince them of what you know about God.*

Then I prayed like I'd never prayed before. In the school the missionaries prayed for us, and we prayed our little prayers, but they never meant much to me. But here on top of the mesa there was nobody to go to, no Christian person near.

During that time at home I had written letters to friends outside, but they never reached the post office, and the letters that came for me never reached me. The people around me seemed to want to hide me for some reason or other, and I didn't have any communication with any Christian person. In the fall before that I had written Mr. Mitchell and had sent the letter out with a prospector. I told him that I would like to go back to school. When Mr. Mitchell received my letter he came right up to find me. But we had moved up to Cocamina Mesa and he couldn't get up there, so he went back. He wrote to another missionary to go out and try to find me, but he waited until February. There was two feet of snow and we were living away up in the canyon and he couldn't find us.

That day on top of the mesa I really prayed. I got down on my knees and asked the Lord to deliver me.

Two days after that we saw a man coming up the ravine, leading a packhorse, and behind him was an Indian boy. The man was Mr. Mitchell, and the little boy was my brother. Mr. Mitchell had been trying to find me. He came out a road where people told him I lived, but the road petered out and he didn't know which way to go. He saw a shepherd boy come over the hill with some sheep and asked him if he knew a girl around there that had been to Tolcheco to school. He said, "Yes, that's my sister." Then they came to the hogan.

I was sitting behind the loom where my mother was weaving. Mr. Mitchell began to talk to her about the gospel and about believing in Christ. She said, "Oh, that's too hard. We just can't follow that way." Then I spoke up and said, "No, mother, it isn't too hard." Then Mr. Mitchell knew that I was the one who was behind the loom.

He made camp and stayed all night. The next morning after I took the sheep and the lambs out I went over to see him. He said to me, "Grace, we have come for you. We have come to take you back to school."

It was sort of a shock. I had been praying for deliverance, and when it came it was sort of a shock to me.

I went back and told my folks that this man wanted to take me back to school. My mother hit the ceiling of the hogan. She was mad. I've never seen her so mad before. She said, "You've broken your promise. You promised that you would stay with us here. You go. Don't think that you have a mother. Just go. Let the missionary be your mother. Let him be your father."

I went down to the well and prayed some more. It just seemed that I had assurance that everything would be all right.

In the morning Mother was all right. She was ready to let me go. She combed my hair for me, and I got on the horse, and the children laughed at me. We rode away, over the hills.

When I was at Ganado, Miss Edgerton came from somewhere, and they told me to go and interpret for her. But that was the last thing that I wanted to do—to interpret—and that was a cross I had to bear for that year. I guess Miss Edgerton knows the tough time I gave her trying to interpret. To this day I can't interpret very well. I guess I don't know the two languages very well, that's the reason.

During that year—whether Miss Edgerton knows it or not—the thought came to me often: *What right have the white people to say that you find salvation through the Bible and Christ? What right have they to say that? Maybe my own people have the right way.*

Then the experience of those eighteen months in the hogan would come to me, and I would say: "There is a God. He brought me through."

If I had listened to Satan during my first year as an

interpreter, I wouldn't be serving God now. But I know that God heard me when I prayed that day on the mesa. I can look back on those things and know that God worked for me.

6

Wooden-Legs

IN SPITE of her feelings of inadequacy, Grace was a faithful helper to Faye, and the two worked as a harmonious team. At the school in Ganado or out visiting in the hogans on the desert, they were good companions. Grace was young and happy and gay—a girl after Faye's own heart. They laughed and wept together.

When an outstation was established in the desolate valley of Cornfields, about twelve miles from Ganado, Faye and Grace were chosen to initiate work in the waterless region. Here and there in the barren wilderness were hogans, surrounded by brush shelters where the Indians cooked and lived in good weather. Poor and unschooled, the people needed all kinds of help. The mission dream was to have a community house where the Indians could come to bathe and sew, and where basic medical needs could be met. By dint of much effort enough building material was assembled to construct a U-shaped building as a start.

The two women, alone at the center, became evangelists and nurses, counselors and teachers. The Navajo neighbors would have to be encouraged to visit the new foreign camp in their valley. They were skeptical.

After a year of arduous pioneering, the work took root as the neighbors were won over by friendliness. They began to learn many new things, such as running a pedal sewing machine. They even began to sample the white man's medicines—secretly and fearfully at first, for the medicine men were still in strong power.

When the center was functioning well, with Grace as Faye's articulate partner in the project, a pattern once familiar to Faye began to appear: eligible young men would visit occasionally, with a special interest in Grace. One of these was Roger Davis, a Navajo who had been trained in Ganado and was now preaching in Chinle, Arizona, where he was proving to be a great help in evangelizing his own people. He was quite a bit older than Grace and had known her as a small, mischievous girl in the mission school.

"I'd known him most of my life," Grace recalls. "He told me later that he thought I was very naughty and many times he wanted to spank me. He was a young man and I was very small. He changed his mind after I grew up, I think."

Grace and Roger were married in a lovely service at Ganado, then went to Chinle, where they would continue serving Christ and their tribe for many years to come.

Faye's new interpreter was only seventeen years old when she went to Cornfields. She was bright and eager, and gave every promise of developing into a good helper. After a short time, however, it became quite apparent that the Christian way of life was too confining for her restless spirit. One night when a squaw dance was in progress nearby, the familiar, haunting Navajo music drifted through the open window and into the girl's attentive ear. The cadence of the songs she had known and the rhythm of the dance were compelling; she had to respond. While Faye slept, her young partner quietly slipped through the window and out to the desert around the campfires where unmarried girls were hopefully dancing.

Faye awoke to find herself once again without an Indian helper.

Needing a change from the parched desiccation of the

Cornfields Valley and the tiring accumulation of disappointments, Faye decided to spend part of the summer of 1925 at a missionary conference in Flagstaff where other workers were gathering. At the foot of the snow-covered San Francisco peaks, among the fragrant pines, she was completely revived and renewed. As she was leaving Flagstaff to return to the challenge of Cornfields, the car she was driving tipped over a steeply graded embankment, pinning Faye under the wheels.

"I would have been killed by the weight of the car on my chest. I began to choke very quickly," she recalled. "When they got the car off of me, they had a prayer meeting right there in the ditch. If I had any bones broken or any internal injuries, they were healed at that time, for the doctors found no injuries."

Soon she was back on the job at Cornfields, "feeling just as well as before the accident." And she added, "I cannot thank God enough for His loving kindness through all of this. He must have work for me yet to do for Him, and my one desire is that I may fulfill all His purpose in thus sparing my life."

Accidents and illness, alternating with periods of intensive labor, became a patterned way of life for Faye. Some had predicted that in view of her past health record, prognosis for a productive future was poor. But her reserve of vitality —for which she always gave God credit—seemed inexhaustible. From every adversity she always sprang back with as much bounce as before.

Later at Cornfields she was joined by Martha Conklin, a mature Navajo woman who was completely dedicated in her desire to evangelize her people. In her remaining years, she worked side by side with Faye at Cornfields, steadily helping in all kinds of tasks, menial or inspiring. There was much hardship: hauling water from the well; cleaning the kerosene lamps; dispensing medicines—after the patients were persuaded to come for them; teaching women to sew; encouraging and evangelizing people to whom the Bible was an exotic new idea.

Faye was constantly frustrated by her inability to speak the language, but Martha was a good and sympathetic communicator. Faye began to take notes on useful phrases and sentences, and she began to learn as she heard certain words repeated. She was curious; she longed for time to study the language which now could only be caught on the fly.

As summer came on, Faye noticed that the people were all asking, "When is Chicken Pull Day?" She learned that this was the Navajo version of the Fourth of July. "When the first traders came out to live among the Navajos," she explained, "they prepared a big celebration for the Indians with various kinds of races, the chief event being the chicken pulling race. In this, a live chicken is buried up to its neck in the ground and then the men ride by on their ponies and see who can pull the chicken out of the ground. Poor chicken! This race was so popular with the Indians that it was always a part of the Fourth of July celebration. Since the traders never took the trouble to tell the people what the day really stands for, the people gradually came to call it Chicken Pull Day."

A week before the celebration, special shelters of cedar and pinyon boughs were set up near the trader's store. One was for sick persons and medicine men who conducted healing ceremonies, and one was for cooking. Boiled mutton, homemade bread, and coffee were given to the Indians who came. Little booths were set up to sell candy, fruit, watermelon, and pop day and night. The crowds grew to large proportions as Indians came to the sings conducted for healing and the squaw dances for matchmaking.

Faye was unhappy with this perversion of the Fourth of July. She wrote to friends: "Here at Cornfields I have put up a big American flag in our meeting room, and am giving short patriotic and historical talks. May the day be hastened when the Chicken Pull will be superseded by a clean, truly patriotic, and Christian celebration of the day that stands for real liberty for all Americans, whether white, black, or red."

Christmas Day was a gay time at the Cornfields community center as Faye and Martha worked hard to make it a memorable occasion for the Navajos. They even managed a Christmas program for which they taught the children to say special pieces and sing Christmas carols. And each was given a bag holding candy, nuts, an apple, and "a big cinnamon roll"—baked by Faye.

"As the sun began to sink," Faye wrote, "they started home over the desert in wagons and on horseback, all happy and impressed."

She had stressed the need for giving as well as receiving, and an offering was taken. One old woman, grateful for what God had done for her, gave fifty cents of a Christmas dollar she had received. "A hundred-pound sack of corn, half a mutton, and a ring brought the total value of the gifts up to fifteen dollars," Faye remembered.

In those days at Cornfields it was impossible to set up a clinic schedule or to arrange for regular meetings, for the people did not know "Tuesday from Thursday." They were not accustomed to the white man's seven-day week. They began to come asking, "When is Sunday?" Gradually this day developed as a point of time orientation. People came and listened closely to the Bible messages that were given. One man, whose name was Left-Hander, came to listen but was unimpressed. His little daughter became ill with pneumonia. When she became too sick to be moved to Ganado hospital, Faye and Martha took her into their home and nursed her for two weeks. Later, both Left-Hander and his wife became sincere believers.

Sometimes the babies Faye medicated did not recover. She said of such cases: "God has often used the death of a little one to bring the parents to Himself. Among the Navajos there is a custom of dealing with stubborn sheep or goats. If the mother sheep will not go where the shepherd desires, he just picks up her little lamb and carries it off in his arms, and then the old sheep follows wherever the shepherd leads. Sometimes here among the Navajos bereaved parents find comfort in the truth that their little ones are in heaven. Recently a couple who had lost two little children started following the Good Shepherd toward the fold to which their little ones had been taken."

Water had been a very big problem in Cornfields. When the community center was first built, there had been the promise of a bathing room and a laundry. As time went by and these did not materialize, word began to be whispered around that the missionary's God did not answer prayer after all. Challenged on this point, the missionaries set aside a week for special prayer directed to God for the supply of the much needed water. Every well that was dug, however, soon filled with quicksand. It seemed impossible to eliminate it. One day, unexpectedly, some government engineers came with their big equipment and set to work. They had heard of the need and had come to help. Within days there was a good supply of water for the center.

Most of the Indians of the area had never seen a bathtub. "The shining new white tub with its hot and cold water and its handy outlet for the dirty water is a marvelous thing!" Faye wrote. "But most of the people have to be shown how to let the water in and out, told to get *in* the tub and sit down, and how to clean it afterward. That is the price of the bath —a clean tub!"

Gradually more and more patients came to the clinic for medicines as their effectiveness was proven. This made for strained relations with the local medicine men, whose incomes began to diminish.

Faye recounted the story of one of their patients who had lost faith in the power of the ceremonial singers to heal: "One Saturday afternoon when Martha and I were finishing our weekly cleaning we heard footsteps on the porch, and the door opened without the preliminary knock. A short middle-aged man with a deeply lined face walked in with a peculiarly stiff gait. After the usual greetings we learned that this man, a stranger to us, had previously lived in Cornfields Valley, but had moved away to Indian Wells. He was back now, and had come for medicine for his sick children. He said that he had no faith in the medicine men since he lost his legs ten years before."

The man, who came to be known as Wooden-Legs, had become involved in a fight while he was drunk. He had been thrown from his horse and had lain in the snow all during one bitterly cold night. His feet had been frozen, and gangrene had set in. All of the best medicine men of the area were called in. They sang and prayed and made many sand paintings, but the man did not recover. Seeing that he was dying, the medicine men fled.

His relatives took him to the government hospital at Keams Canyon, where his legs were amputated and his life saved. While he was convalescing some of his fellow tribesmen who had believed the gospel visited him and told him of Christ. Later some of the evangelists from Ganado told him more when he returned to his home in Indian Wells. A gospel team had gone to the big nine-day *yeibichai*. These are ceremonies conducted for the healing of the sick, but many persons not ill also attend. As these Navajos talked to groups who would listen to their message, Wooden-Legs overheard what they were saying. He began to think about Christ's invitation to come to Him for eternal life.

Faye and Martha told him more of the Bible message that Saturday afternoon, and he was quite ready to accept Christ.

"He knelt down on his creaky wooden legs and gratefully accepted Christ that day," Faye wrote.

A few weeks later he brought his wife to hear about his Savior. He had already talked to her, and she was also ready to receive Him, but she was afraid to try to pray. She was steeped in the belief of her people that prayers had to be said just right, as the medicine men did, or they did no good. She was fearful.

"Finally she got the idea that she could just talk to the Lord," Faye recounted, "and she asked Him to come into her heart."

The next year Wooden-Legs and his family moved up into the hills where they were hard to reach during the winter season. Toward spring their youngest child, a three-year-old girl, ate some poison put out for the coyotes and became very ill. Wooden-Legs came to Cornfields for medicine, but it was too late. Before long, word reached Faye that the child had died. Wooden-Legs was heartbroken. And none of his relatives would help him dig the grave because they blamed him for the death of his child. It was his fault, they said, for he had become a Christian.

Wooden-Legs dug the grave alone and buried his little girl. As soon as Faye and Martha heard about it they found their way to Wooden-Legs' home to encourage and comfort him and his wife. He told them that while he was digging the grave he had no fear. He knew that he was not really alone, because the presence of Christ was a reality to him.

Through many other testings, and in the face of much opposition from relatives, Wooden-Legs stood true to his faith in Christ, never wavering.

7

Let Us Eat and Be Married

FOR FIVE WINTERS, as the Navajos count time, Faye and Martha weathered the alternate sun and wind and snow which marked the seasons in Cornfields Valley. A resolute little flock of Christians had learned the meaning of Sunday, and people were coming from great distances to hear the Good Story and sing the few Christian hymns that existed in their language.

In 1930 the white man's depression had begun to affect missions on the reservation, and the diminishing dollars of donated funds had to do double duty. Personnel at Ganado was reduced, and strict economy measures were applied to keep the school and hospital functioning. Faye, asked to pinch-hit at Ganado, had to leave the work at Cornfields.

One regret was that her faithful partner, Martha, would not be going with her. Lame from birth, Martha found her handicap becoming more serious. It would no longer be possible for her to walk as she and Faye had done for five years in the rugged valley, telling her people of Christ. "It will be hard to find another helper as earnest as she," Faye wrote.

Duties back at Ganado were a sharp change from visiting scattered hogans on the desert. Now Faye was supervising the girls' dormitory and the hospital kitchen, and working with educated young people. Excerpts from her letters reveal her involvement in a variety of jobs, matched always by her unfailing versatility:

"At present I'm trying to mother 60 girls—30 little ones and 30 intermediates! It is an impossible task and only God's grace and strength enable anyone to carry it. But I do love the children—interesting, if trying!"

In 1931 when the financial pinch was severest and the closing of the school and hospital seemed imminent, Faye wrote:

"The workers, realizing what this would mean in the lives of the children—not only loss of school and Christian influences but real privation in many homes—pledged their salaries for three months. This, with the closing of four buildings, crowding the work into the rest, and very strict economy of light, heat, and workers' food, raised almost enough money to meet the estimated deficit."

At Christmas time Faye could not deny herself the joy of returning to Cornfields to visit her friends there. "This was a special joy to me," she wrote, "for it was like going home to meet my own children in the Lord again."

So successful had been her pioneering in Cornfields that in 1932 she was asked to organize a community center and hogan-visiting program in White Earth, a bleak little out-post eight miles west of the Arizona-New Mexico state line. Known to the white people as Allantown, it was in a poor area, filled with Navajos who suffered many kinds of hard-ship. Medical work was heavy, especially following a severe winter in 1932. She noted that "the strong survive, but the weak suffer, not only from their illnesses but from the prac-tices of medicine men. They keep the sick person (who should be resting) awake all night chanting their prayers to the spirits. They sometimes give strong herb drinks, or ad-vise sweat baths which may or may not be helpful in a particular case."

People would come from long distances to seek aid in severe cases where medicine men had failed. Faye wrote of one:

"A young man walked some eight or ten miles across coun-try to ask us to come and get a woman who had tried to kill herself the night before. His camp was fifteen miles by road up in the hills and the road was very bad, but we could not refuse to make an attempt at least to reach the woman. We were very thankful that we got stuck only once on the way. Finally we reached the camp and found a typical small hogan of logs and mud. An open fire was burning on the dirt floor under the hole in the center of the roof. A packing box made a cupboard for some cooking utensils. A saddle, another box or two, and some sheepskins here and there on the floor completed the furnishings. On one side of the fire sat a middle-aged man with a troubled face, evidently the husband of the woman we had come for. A couple of young men sat near him while on the other side a capable-looking young woman knelt beside a woman half sitting, half lying on a pile of sheepskins. Her head was wrapped in a grimy cloth and her sateen waist was bloody; her face was thin, pale, and haggard.

"After we had shaken hands all around and sat down on the proffered sheepskin, the husband told us what had happened. His wife had been sick for some time with what they said was a sore throat. We found later that it was an advanced case of tuberculosis. Four days before that she had had a baby, and it had died the second night. He had been taking care of her at night, but one night he was so tired he had dozed off. While he slept the woman had slipped out and had hit her head seven times with the ax! They were afraid she might try to kill herself again, or harm someone else, and they were anxious for us to take her somewhere for help. She was willing to go.

"We took her to the Christian Reformed Mission Hospital five miles east of Gallup. On the way we told her of Jesus' love, and of His desire to help her now. She replied that the words were good. We don't know how much she understood, for she was very sick and died three weeks later.

"Suicide is most unusual among the Navajos, and we were anxious to find out the real reason why she tried to take her life. We discovered that within the last three years she had lost her mother and a brother and a sister. Her husband was cruel to her, often beating her. Surely enough to make anyone desperate!"

There was encouragement in the Sunday meetings at the center where Navajos would come from distant hogans to

hear the Good Story. The older people could understand
only in their own language, and many of the young people,
including those who had been to school, preferred hearing
the Bible lessons in Navajo. Faye mentioned that at that
time about eighty percent of the people of the tribe understood no English.

During the years of growing activity in the community
center at White Earth, Faye was evaluating the needs of
The People. There were many calls for help, too many for
a few workers to handle. She remembered the strong Korean
Christians and began to dream of an equally strong body
of Navajo believers. Observing the students returning from
government schools, she began to envision future leaders
from among The People themselves, those who would bear
the burden for their own tribe. She accordingly helped
organize a Returned Students Club to foster the further-
ance of their education at home, with a view to the training
of Christian leaders.

Although the trend of education, even in missions, was
strongly directed toward the use of English, Faye observed
the inevitable warm response of people to hymns, messages,
and portions of Scripture translated into Navajo. She was
bothered and embarrassed by the lack of a complete New
Testament in the language, and the inadequate communication of God's Word through interpreters. Extemporaneous
translations of the Bible often mystified or misled the listen-
ers. Once she wrote:

"I remember one fine young man who was interpreting
a message on the prodigal son. When the missionary told of
the father's word, 'Bring hither the fatted calf and kill it;
let us eat and be merry,' the interpreter said, 'Let us eat and
be *married*'!

"I longed to have the translation of the New Testament
finished and more of the people able to read it, for I re-

membered so clearly what I had seen the Word in their own language do for the Korean people. All of this troubled me, and although I tried to learn the language as I had done in Korea, there was no time given for this as in a foreign field."

8

Yellow-at-the-Edge-of-the-Woods

OFTEN ALONE at White Earth, without the companionship of other missionaries, Faye would pray—and dream. She envisioned schools where capable Navajo young people would receive Bible training in their own language; she dreamed of churches manned by intelligent, eloquent Navajo preachers.

She was unaware that not far away others were sharing her dreams, and that several mission leaders were bringing the vision to earth at Fort Defiance.

In 1935 a new venture under the direction of Howard Clark was launched, an effort in which several denominations were cooperating to train Navajo Christian leaders. The new organization would meet the need for "trained native leadership" and "Navajo language study for missionaries." Within a short time Faye made arrangements to join the staff of the Navajo Bible Training School, as the group was called. (It later became the Navajo Bible School and Mission.)

When the school opened on January 31, the first meal was "a fine turkey dinner cooked under the direction of Miss Edgerton"! She was also the matron of the girls attending the school. Her musical ability was helpful in training the choir and in teaching music to the prospective Christian leaders.

Her chief delight, however, was the study of the Navajo language and teaching the students to read Bible portions which had been translated by early missionaries. Although these consisted of only a few portions, at least it was a beginning, a step toward the desired goal. This booklet of Scripture portions was "a blessing to those who read it—but so few could read it." The alphabet used was very difficult.

In 1937 Faye responded to the call for someone to go to an encampment named Pine Springs, to nurture a potential indigenous church. Perched among the pines on the crest of a high, windswept hill, Pine Springs was far from any mission influence, an ideal location to begin teaching Navajos to take the responsibility for their own services.

Faye lived at first in a little log cabin which the wild wind at times seemed to try to wrest from its rocky moorings. Later Mr. Clark arranged to have a small house trailer moved up on the hill for her home.

The first few Christians were as hardy as the tenacious pine trees—they were often buffeted by strong opposing winds, and their roots were driven deep. It was incomparable bliss for Faye to be teaching these stalwart Navajos and at last to be learning the language herself. But the same old struggle with the written language persisted. It was hard to teach people to read.

Later Faye was to learn the reason for the struggle with the language, and she wrote: "The first missionaries who translated and wrote the language were not linguists, and they had not recognized that the language was tonal. Neither had they learned that the length of vowels often makes the difference in the meanings of words." Thus there was much ambiguity and misunderstanding in the reading of the

Scripture portions in the first orthography. Even so, the struggle was rewarding; Navajos learned much more from these portions of the Bible in their own language than they did from King James English.

Faye's need for a language helper and companion was met in 1937 when Mr. Clark arranged for a mature teen-ager, Dorothy Silversmith, to go to Pine Springs. Dorothy had been graduated from the eighth grade of the Christian Reformed mission school at Rehoboth near Gallup and, according to the letter describing her, was eager to serve God and help her own people. Faye was to meet her new companion at the trading post at Houck, on the main highway. Mail came every other day, and the mail truck was Faye's only transportation. She arranged to go out on the next trip of the truck, after receiving the letter.

Meanwhile a composed but somewhat confused and lonely Navajo teen-ager arrived at the trading post on July 9, 1937, with no one to meet her. She had come by bus from her home near Continental Divide—"the longest ride I ever had," she remembered. She had never been so far from home, and she had no idea what awaited her at her destination. She only knew that she was to go and help Miss Edgerton, whom she had never met.

Poised and self-possessed, the young girl did not betray her disappointment and loneliness to the kind friends at the trading post who provided hospitality the night she arrived. The next day, however, she was relieved when the mail truck pulled up to the trading post and "a little white lady about *so tall* got out," Dorothy recalled, indicating Faye's height. "I thought she was *cute!*"

Faye immediately loved and admired the independent, self-reliant Navajo girl. Thus began an enduring friendship which deepened through long years of association.

The bus Dorothy boarded was within sight of her mother's land, Yellow-at the-Edge-of-the-Woods. There Dorothy was born into her mother's Grand Canyon Clan, and there she tended sheep as a small child. She was the daughter of Little Horn, a conservative Navajo who loved the old ways of his people and resented the encroachment of the white man, whose ways he did not trust.

In the morning Dorothy was always awakened by the sound of her father's voice singing to greet the dawn. He would go outside the hogan, face the east, and toss a pinch of corn pollen eastward as he sang. Dorothy would follow him with her little buckskin bag of pollen and dutifully mimic the motions of her father. This was the right way; this would insure a good, happy day and would keep them from misfortune. Shivering in the morning chill, she would then take her lambs out to the pasture.

Later, when the sun was higher in the sky, she would come back to the hogan and eat the savory mutton stew her mother made, or perhaps just Indian fried bread and coffee. Soon she was off again, running like a young deer over the yellow earth where her sheep were hunting for tufts of green grass. She carried with her a bag of *naneskaadi,* the fried bread that tasted so good when one was hungry. All day long, until the sun was low in the sky, she would follow her sheep.

When she was still quite small her brother was born. She loved him dearly, and when he could be carried she took him with her as she watched the sheep.

At night after the sheep were safely in the corral she loved the warm glow of the fire inside the hogan. In the winter when the wind howled outside, it was pleasant to sit on the big woolly sheepskin and listen to her father tell stories about the old days. He told stories of his father, Big Horn, who suffered on the Long March when the Navajo people were taken captive and corraled like sheep or goats. Her grandfather had other enemies, too, almost as bad as the white men. The Utes were very mean, and they stole the cows of the Navajos. There were other groups of Plains Indians who made war with Big Horn and his people.

Dorothy loved the stories, and she learned from her father a deep love and loyalty to her own people and their ways. There was comfort and security in the hogan set firmly on the land of the Grand Canyon Clan.

One night Dorothy was sitting beside her mother on the sheepskin, watching the fire dance and throw shadows on the far wall of the hogan. Little Horn had finished telling his tale and had fallen asleep. It was quiet, so quiet that one could hear the small noises the fire was making.

Suddenly Dorothy began to cry softly, and big tears rolled down her chubby cheeks.

"Why are you crying, little girl?" asked her mother.

"I—I don't know," sobbed the child.

And Dorothy really didn't know why, except that she was very sad. She could not put into Navajo words the sadness she felt, because she was thinking about death, and how lonely it would be to die. She had once seen a lamb die, and she had cried. Now suddenly the thought of the lamb's dying had flashed through her childish memory as she watched the fire, and she cried without wanting to.

What happened to you when you died? She had seen her neighbors move out of their hogan after a family member's death, and there stood the lonesome home, with no one in it and a big hole knocked through the north wall as a sign that someone had died. But where was the person who once lived in that hogan?

Dorothy was afraid, and she snuggled up close to her mother on the sheepskin. It was one of her earliest memories, and she never forgot it.

No one in Dorothy's family had ever gone to the white man's school, but Little Horn decided that she should learn to read and write. She was sent to live with an older brother who was married and lived near a government school. Dorothy was not happy, however, because her brother drank and there was trouble in his home. Later she attended a Christian Reformed mission school at Rehoboth, twenty-five miles away. Her parents had heard that the missionaries were good to the children and taught them well.

Before Dorothy left for the school, however, her mother talked much with her about how to behave and what to do at the white man's school where they would try to teach her another way, another religion. She told her to close her ears, not to listen when the white people talked about their gods.

"Just learn to read and write—but don't listen when they want you to leave the Navajo way. We have our own religion, and that is for us Navajos. It's better for us than the white man's way. Just don't pay any attention when they talk," she told Dorothy.

Dorothy did as her mother had told her and did not pay attention to the missionaries' talk; it was all around her, but she did not let it get inside her. However, she couldn't help noticing the picture of the Good Shepherd on the wall of the dormitory. She saw it every time she went to her room. The face of the Shepherd was kind and loving. She didn't know much about the Navajo gods, but they weren't like that. And the God the missionaries talked about was good and wise and powerful. He loved all people. He loved the Navajo people.

The picture of the Good Shepherd carrying a lamb made a lasting impression on Dorothy. That Shepherd was Jesus, seeking for people to be His sheep.

When school was out Dorothy went back to her home at Yellow-at-the-Edge-of-the-Woods where her own woolly lambs were waiting for her. There were new lambs, too, and she was given the job of shepherding the very small ones who needed special watching. All day long she followed them over the hills and down the ravines, stopping when she was hungry to eat her *naneskaadi*.

One day she came home as usual at sundown and herded

the lambs into the corral. Suddenly she realized that one was missing. Without going into the hogan to tell her mother, she turned right around and went out to find it. She tried to think where it might be.

How did I lose it? she wondered. *Where could it be? Is it down in the gully or up on the hill?*

As she looked and searched, wondering where the lamb was, she remembered that the God the missionaries prayed to knows *everything;* He would know where the lamb was.

There on the yellow earth, as darkness was falling, she prayed for the first time in her life to God in heaven. She asked Him to help her find her lamb.

And He answered her prayer. As she walked along, she saw in her mind's eye a clump of bushes at a certain spot on the desert.

Maybe that's where my lamb is, she thought.

She went to the clump and there lay the lamb under a bush. It allowed her to pick it up and carry it. That was a miracle to Dorothy, for the lambs would often run away and not let her catch them.

With a happy heart she started home with the lamb in her arms. The moon was now up, climbing the sky. It lightened the path and the bushes all the way to the hogan in the distance. Suddenly Dorothy remembered the picture on the wall of the dormitory, and she thought, *Jesus wants me. He wants to find me. He wants me to be His lamb.*

She knelt again with the lamb in her arms, the full moon shining down on her. She asked the Good Shepherd to take her for His lamb.

It was a real transaction in the heart of the little Navajo girl.

Dorothy did not tell her mother or father what had happened, but they noticed a change in her. And very soon they began to call her *enishoodi,* missionary.

She returned to school and told her teachers that she

wanted to study about the Good Shepherd and she wanted to make a confession of her faith. They taught her the catechism in the Dutch tradition of the school, although memorizing in English was very difficult for her. She persevered until she mastered it, then was baptized and joined the church. Her faith was strong from the beginning, and she never wavered.

In the school Dorothy was obedient and hardworking. She was neat in her appearance—except for her black hair, which seemed to resist any taming and often looked disheveled, even when she had tried to comb it.

The kids called her Buffalo, because her hair was always sticking up. But she just laughed with them, because it was true.

As Dorothy matured, her Christian conviction deepened, and with it came a strong desire to teach her own people. One verse of Scripture had been engraved upon her heart, Ephesians 2:6: "By grace are ye saved through faith, and that not of yourselves, it is *the gift of God*."

That is what she thought about, that "gift of God." She wanted her people to know that.

One day while talking to a mission leader she mentioned that she wanted to preach to her own people.

"You can't *preach*—you're a woman, and women don't preach," was the firm Dutch answer.

She was really upset about that. *Why do I have to be a woman?* she thought. *I want so much for my tribe to know about God's gift for them.*

After graduation from the school she went back to Yellow-at-the-Edge-of-the-Woods, wondering what the future held. She was unlike other Navajo girls her age, whose thoughts were only on marriage and children. Dorothy knew that this was not for her; she wanted to serve the Lord.

One day a man from the Rehoboth mission appeared at

her mother's hogan and asked to see Dorothy. While waiting for her to be summoned, the white man chatted with
Little Horn. The foreigner was not quite prepared for the
tirade which struck his ears. Dorothy's father was outspoken
in his lack of confidence in the white people. They were
only spies for the government, he declared—all of them.
They were not to be trusted. Missionaries were no excep-
tion. The mission leader wondered how Dorothy had weathered such strong opposition to the ideas which she embraced.
She was truly an independent spirit, he concluded, with
strong personal convictions.

The missionary finally had a word alone with Dorothy.
He asked her, "Do you still want to serve God?"

"Yes," was the firm reply.

"Well, go to Rehoboth, and they will tell you how to
get to Houck. There is a missionary, Miss Edgerton, who
wants a helper."

Dorothy, not knowing where she was going, got on the
bus and took the long ride.

9

A Turn in the Road

"DOROTHY WAS a little impatient about teaching me the
language," Faye recalled with a wry smile. "It's hard to
teach somebody who just stumbles along. She'd much rather
just say it for me than help me say it."

Dorothy's impatience was accentuated by the fact that
Faye was one of the first white woman missionaries to make
a serious attempt at learning the difficult language. A few

white men had learned to speak it, and those existing portions of the Bible in Navajo had been translated by men. Heavy work on the language, and particularly Bible translation, was considered a man's job. Men were theologically trained and educationally equipped for such work; it was appropriately their role. Nor had Faye considered the possibility of translation activity; she was only anxious to communicate with the people for herself rather than use the accepted way, through an interpreter. Because of the struggle, Dorothy wondered about the efficiency of Faye's efforts. Perhaps it would be simpler for *her* to do the talking!

"Dorothy was very zealous for the Lord, and she longed to see her people believe in Him," Faye remembered. And Dorothy soon began to make an impression upon her own tribesmen in Pine Springs. Her teaching was sincere and emphatic; she urged the people to believe in Christ for salvation. At last she was "preaching" about the gift of God which had changed her life, beginning that memorable night she had knelt on the yellow earth and talked to the Good Shepherd.

So effective was her evangelism that people began to believe her message, and they came inquiring for more Bible teaching.

"When the medicine men and other tribal leaders realized what we were really teaching, they wanted to put us out, although we had not tried to arouse their opposition," Faye wrote. "They planned a community meeting on a certain day to discuss the matter. They were about to decide to tell us to leave.

"The day before the meeting was to be held, the man leading the opposition got drunk and was put in jail. There was no meeting, and we were not asked to go."

The following year Faye and Dorothy extended their evangelistic efforts to Crystal, the settlement Faye had once visited at Christmastime. In that high, cold mountainous region was "a little nucleus of believers" asking for more teaching. There they taught the children in the government school and held Christian meetings for the people on Sundays and Wednesdays. It was in Crystal that Faye made her first efforts to teach people to read by making "a crude attempt at a primer." She felt keenly her lack not only of training in the language but also of methods for teaching adults to read.

In spite of the obstacles, she and Dorothy valiantly used the primer and the charts Faye had made, and they were encouraged by the response of a number who eagerly tried to learn to read. There was a visible hunger for reading the Word of God.

In the winter of 1940 Faye and Dorothy were asked to help in the Navajo training school which had now moved from Fort Defiance to Window Rock. Mr. Clark and his staff were in the process of building a permanent center for training Navajo workers. The housing was as yet inadequate, and the winter was severe.

"That first winter was *cold*," Dorothy recalls. "The snow came in on our beds, right between the boards of the walls. Miss Edgerton and those other missionaries were *real* pioneers in those days!"

The physical hardships at Window Rock were of slight consequence to Faye compared with matters of greater concern pressing daily upon her. Although delighted with the goal of endeavoring to establish indigenous churches and training young Navajos to direct them, she keenly sensed the lack of Navajo Scriptures needed as a basis for their training. English was simply not understood by many of the students.

Faye kept praying for *someone* to finish the translation, "but there seemed to be no one to go ahead with it. One older missionary was working at it a little in the few hours he could spare out of a busy schedule of 'regular missionary activities.' "

In the early years of missionary labor on the reservation both Protestant and Catholic workers had concentrated on writing the language. Fred Mitchell compiled a handbook on Navajo. This and the Franciscan Fathers' *Ethnological Dictionary* were among the first materials to be published. Later L. P. Brink, a Christian Reformed missionary, prepared a hymnbook and translated Genesis and Mark. These two books of the Bible were published in 1910 by The American Bible Society. John Butler and Alexander Black, Presbyterian missionaries, also mastered the language and translated short portions of the Scriptures. In 1917 portions from Exodus, Psalms, Luke, Romans, First Corinthians, and Revelation, together with revised versions of Genesis and Mark, appeared in one volume. This was a cooperative effort of the four men who had previously worked independently. In 1935 the book of Acts was added to this volume, which was republished and entitled *God Bizaad*—God's Word.

Not only had nothing more been published, but practically no Bible translation was in process.

When Faye expressed her deep desire to be given time for language study with a view to using effectively the portions in print, one mission leader said, "On rainy days you can work on the language."

"But there were so *few* rainy days in that dry climate!" Faye lamented.

In 1942 a young couple from California, Turner and Helen Blount, appeared at Window Rock. They had come with a desire to use the language in evangelism, and for that purpose had taken a course at the Summer Institute of Linguistics, a new venture under the direction of Cameron Townsend. Soon Faye was chatting with them about the language. Although Turner had not yet studied the language on location, he had learned the sounds of the alphabet and knew a few words. Faye challenged his pronunciation of a few sounds.

"I think you're *hearing* things!" laughed Faye incredulously.

"Well, that's the way they taught us over at the Summer Institute," said Turner with a chuckle. "Maybe you'd better go over and take the course—and check it out yourself."

Faye did not forget the challenge. She became curious about the new school for linguists and later recalled, "My interest was aroused, and I thought about attending."

The following year Faye found herself in the company of a group of budding missionary-linguists under the direction of Drs. Kenneth L. Pike and Eugene A. Nida on the campus of Bacone College in Muskogee, Oklahoma. There she learned the principles of linguistic analysis and received intensive drill in sounds of languages from around the world —including the odd sounds in Navajo which Turner had learned to make even before going to the Navajo field.

She heard also that Drs. Edward Sapir and Harry Hoijer had done considerable work on Navajo and their findings were being published.

A new day had dawned for Faye, and she was overjoyed. A brand-new realization gradually began to formulate itself in her thinking, a possibility hitherto not considered by her, at least. Pike and Nida had encouraged all of the neophytic linguists to believe that *they*, with training and consultation, could translate the Scriptures. This included Faye.

"I enjoyed the course and learned a lot," Faye remembered. "I returned to the mission full of enthusiasm to help further the translation in Navajo."

Back at the school in Window Rock a full schedule of activities began to fill her hours once more—hospital and hogan visitation, teaching classes of reading and music, helping occasionally in the kitchen—there was no time for study of the language.

One day in 1944 when her director was planning for a future schedule for the mission workers he asked Faye, "And what do you want to do?"

To his surprise she answered, "I want to do translation work."

With a laugh, and perhaps not too seriously, he said, "Perhaps you should work with the Wycliffe Translators!"

"I hadn't thought about joining Wycliffe," Faye recollected. "But that gave me an idea. I had thought of continuing with the mission, but hoping that time would be given me to work on translation."

The matter was dropped—but not for long.

"I went home and prayed about it for two days," Faye said. "Then I went to my director and told him that I was going to join the Wycliffe Bible Translators."

10

Indians—and Cowboys

"OUR GOD is a God of wonders," Faye wrote home in October, 1944. "He has led me on and given me the opportunity to do the thing that I feel He has been calling me to do for some time. He Himself has brought me to work with the Wycliffe Bible Translators."

The first commandment under Wycliffe was to learn to speak the Indian language well—an order not grievous to Faye, who for years had wanted to do just that. And what better location than Dorothy's own homeland, Yellow-at-the-Edge-of-the-Woods? Although Dorothy had elected to continue working at Window Rock, she cordially invited Faye to join her home circle near Continental Divide.

Faye was in her glory as the little old-fashioned house trailer with its tiny woodburning stove was hauled up the steep highway and over the bumpy dirt road to the expanse of yellow earth which belonged to the Grand Canyon Clan. The trailer came to rest in a "small sunny open space among the pinyon trees, from which there are glorious views in all directions. From the north the high, red cliffs face us, their flat, irregular tops edged with a line of green which seems to emphasize the rose-red of the cliffs, and the matchless blue of the New Mexico sky. This is almost at 'Top-o'-the-World,' the Continental Divide, and at this altitude at night the stars seem almost close enough for one to reach out and take a handful of them! And God seems closer than ever before, too. This is good, for I am living alone, except for my neighbors in the hogans nearby."

Old Little Horn was living alone because his wife was in the tuberculosis sanatorium in Albuquerque. Like so many Navajos, she had been affected by the rigorous climate which often produced lung disorders. Dorothy's sister, Ada, and her husband, Tom, were living in a neighboring hogan. Her small children helped Faye learn the language.

"I am here to immerse myself in the Navajo language," Faye wrote, "looking forward to translation work. God has answered the prayer of many years in allowing me to live thus where no English is spoken. I am depending on Him and your prayers for me, that I may master this language, conceded to be one of the most difficult in the world."

She had many voluntary informants around her constantly, all eager to teach her how to talk.

"Even little Marie, three years old, has caught the idea. The other day I asked her what she had said about a picture she was looking at. She came and stood right in front of me, repeating what she had said very slowly and very earnestly. The only trouble is, she can't quite make all the difficult sounds of Navajo yet herself!

"Sometimes I just sit on a sheepskin on the dirt floor of a hogan, and listen. Usually I take my little 3×5 slips of paper along and write down all I can. Then I have to spend hours analyzing and filing and learning what I have written."

As she plunged into linguistic study, with great determination to absorb everything she heard her neighbors say, there were moments of discouragement, followed by times of elation when she would declare: "I do believe that we shall see His glory among these people through His Word in their hands and hearts some day."

In her fervor to master their mother tongue Faye never forgot that the Indian informants living around her were people who struggled against physical hardships and unseen heartaches. When Tom's old father became ill, she took Tom and Ada to visit the old man whose hogan was about twelve miles away. He had suffered a stroke but was being "cured" by a Navajo ceremony which she described as follows:

"When we arrived we found them in the midst of a medicine man's ceremony. I went in with Ada and watched for a short time. How my heart ached for these people! Tom explained to me that the medicine man was praying to heaven and that this prayer was 'just like ours.' Clothed only in a loin-cloth, the sick old man was held up by two of his sons and made to walk around the fire in the center of the hogan. Then another son bathed him in holy water, and made him kneel while he washed his hair in the same water. Then they spread cornmeal all over his body, and last of all they sprinkled him with the sacred corn pollen, the symbol of life. They said that this afternoon the medicine man was going to make the idols talk. I plan to go over later and see the old man again when he is alone."

While Faye forged ahead at her lonely linguistic outpost, the Blounts were seeking out a place to concentrate on language study. They had also decided to join Wycliffe and focus their efforts upon translating the Bible. Providentially they had met some hospitable friends in Farmington, New Mexico, who invited them to live on the grounds of the Navajo Methodist Mission School. It proved to be a good language-learning situation for the initial stages of their work.

When the winter began to be dangerously severe for Faye in her trailer at Continental Divide, the Blounts suggested that she join them at the mission, where accommodations for her were available. She accepted the offer, exchanging board and room for the teaching of Navajo reading to students of the school three times a week. The situation was certainly more comfortable than the frigid loneliness of her trailer, but Faye missed her contact with the people in their hogans. She soon longed to live near Navajo families where she could hear the language constantly and visit and chat with them in a natural living context.

She discovered that at the edge of the town there was a small no-luxury tourist court, "the only place in Farmington where the Navajos can get rooms for overnight." Soon she was living in the Cowboy Tourist Court, in "one room, about 15' × 15', upstairs in an old adobe house. There are three rooms facing on the porch with an outside stairway, rather rickety and uneven but with a handrail. Navajo young women who work here in town live in the other rooms, and many Navajos come here to stay overnight. That is the reason I chose to live here—that I might have contact with the Navajos. I believe it is going to work out very well, for already one of the young women has come to visit with me and is willing to talk Navajo with me. (Some educated Navajos won't try to talk their language with a white person!)

"The couple who own the place are old-timers here. He is a typical old cowboy, but refined and dignified." She further commented on the frontier flavor of the town that was just beginning to boom with the discovery of oil in the nearby fields. All kinds of fortune seekers were beginning to arrive. These, added to the local cowboys who frequented the town, especially on weekends, converted the historic Indian center into a typical town of the Old West.

The owner of the Cowboy Tourist Court was the proud possessor of several palomino horses. These he loved and cared for as if they were members of the family. One day when one of the cherished animals became acutely ill, he administered a potion concocted of turpentine and other ingredients. The horse recovered.

Later when the owner himself became ill, he thought his condition would be aided by a similar remedy. Without consulting local physicians he doctored himself—with tragic results. Quite suddenly he died.

Just before his death he had expressed one desire: that his favorite song, "I'm Heading for the Last Roundup," be played at his funeral.

Faye was a musician, and it fell to her sad lot to play the little pump organ at "perhaps the largest funeral ever held in Farmington—about two thousand people attending." They stood outside the Cowboy Tourist Court, paying their last respects to a beloved pioneer. Rather apologetically, but deferring loyally to the wish of her deceased landlord, Faye had complied with his request.

Mourning friends remember a small, erect figure vigor-

ously pumping the small organ as the strains of the old cowboy's dirge floated out over Farmington and down into the
canyon below where the San Juan River flowed.

11

Home Between-the-Waters

FARMINGTON WAS the white man's name for it, but it was
not the white man's land.

Long before white men and cowboys overran it, it was
the land of The People.

Long before foreigners began to confine the trees and the
plants to little corrals, making them march in straight rows
where the water ran at their feet; long before big iron
tongues began to suck up the thick black liquid from the
stomach of the earth; long before these things of the white
man began to appear, this was the home of The People.

The People called it Totah, Between-the-Waters. It was
grazing land for their sheep, and it lay between two rivers.
The Spaniards named one river San Juan, and the other
they called Animas.

But there was something about Totah which was more
Navajo than anything else. To the north a few miles, rising
majestically from the flat floor of the desert, was a monument of The People which had not been placed there by
any white man or by any one of The People. It existed
long before any man came to live in this part of the earth.

The monument was called Shiprock by white men, but
to The People it was the Rock with Wings. Long ago it

had come from the heavens and had landed on the earth to show The People where they should live.

With words to match the beauty of this geological master-piece, Willa Cather described the rock-mountain sacred to the Navajos:

And north of the Canyon de Chelly was the Shiprock, a slender crag rising to a dizzy height, all alone out on a flat desert. Seen at a distance of fifty miles or so, that crag presents the figure of a one-masted fishing-boat under full sail, and the white man named it accordingly. But the Indian has another name; he believes that rock was once a ship of the air. Ages ago . . . that crag had moved through the air, bearing upon its summit the parents of the Navajo race from the place in the far north where all peoples were made,—and wherever it sank to earth was to be their land. It sank in a desert country, where it was hard for men to live. But they had found the Canyon de Chelly, where there was shelter and unfailing water. That canyon and the Shiprock were like kind parents . . . places more sacred to them than churches, more sacred than any place is to the white man.*

The mighty rock resting peacefully within sight of Farmington seemed to foreshadow also a dwelling place for the Navajo translation team—and for one member of it in particular, who had long searched for a good place to live with The People.

When Cameron Townsend visited Faye and the Blounts in 1944 he heartily approved of this location where Indians, as well as other missionaries, welcomed the Wycliffe team. Thus the North America Branch of Wycliffe was born in Farmington. This was the first of a number of teams who would translate for North American Indian tribes.

Delighted with her surroundings at the Cowboy Court,

* *Death Comes for the Archbishop* (New York: Alfred A. Knopf, 1946), p. 295.

Faye was in her glory devoting full time to study of the language. Dr. Eugene Nida, then dividing his time between Wycliffe and the American Bible Society, piloted Faye in her early linguistic activities. He had suggested that she try her translation wings by revising the Gospel of Mark which had been published many years earlier. This she did, with the help of two Navajo Christians, Mary Lowe and Geronimo Martin. During the winter of 1945 she wrote: "The revision of Mark is my particular work just now, along with long hours of analysis and research in order to do the work well." She constantly appreciated the published studies of Sapir and Hoijer which enabled her to grasp the grammatical structure of Navajo. "God, in His grace," she wrote, "had led these scientists to do this time-consuming work so that the translation of His Word might be accomplished more rapidly."

As she worked on the revision with Geronimo, she found that he was a brilliant, capable translation partner, and she was delighted. She wrote Dr. Nida: "The prospects for my winter's work are very bright and I do praise the Lord for it all."

Faye had met Geronimo in 1944 when he was in the hospital at Fort Defiance as a patient. He was afflicted with an incurable eye disease and was almost totally blind. Faye, with Turner Blount, was visiting the patients.

"I interpreted for Mr. Blount one afternoon," Geronimo recalled. "Miss Edgerton helped me with the interpretation. I left out a statement that Mr. Blount had made, and Miss Edgerton supplied it for me."

He was impressed with her knowledge of Navajo and her desire to learn more.

As he heard of plans to complete the translation of the New Testament, he was intrigued with the challenge and wanted to help in the project. His keen mind and good memory, augmented by a high school education and thorough knowledge of the Bible, made him a choice candidate for membership on the translation team.

On one occasion in their early association Faye and Geronimo had a sharp difference of opinion. They were both strong-minded individuals, and neither could easily concede points in an argument.

"I got rather cross," Geronimo said, "and she scolded me. She told me that I was proud, and that God could not use me if I was not humble. I admired her for saying that. I appreciated it and it helped me."

Faye was sensitive regarding Christian humility, for she also had been tempted. She judged herself in the same spirit in which she had admonished Geronimo. Not long afterward she found it necessary to ask a fellow missionary to forgive her for the same type of offense. She wrote to the one whom she had offended: "I want to humbly beg your forgiveness, both for the attitude of heart, and the words. Being of an intense and vehement nature, and very proud, I have always found it hard to allow other people to have their own opinions. This comes from the root of pride, I know. I am very glad that the Lord is and has been patiently teaching me the awfulness of the sin of pride, whether it be racial, mental, or spiritual. Great peace has filled my heart since I decided to confess this sin to you."

Faye and Geronimo became close friends and worked together in harmony during the following ten years as they translated the New Testament. Others helped them from time to time, but Geronimo was to become her right arm in the long arduous task. He learned to read in Braille and became a diligent student of the English Bible. They worked side by side in solving many problems involved in translating difficult spiritual concepts into acceptable Navajo.

Recounting the events of his life which had prepared him for this special work, Geronimo said that he "came to know the Lord not instantly, but gradually." He was born in a settlement called Red Mesa, within sight of the Navajo landmark, Shiprock. His father owned a trading post, a building with four rooms. Geronimo recalls that in one of the rooms there were stacks of canned goods and flour, while in another there were stacks of hides—hides of goats and sheep and cows.

Missionaries in the area would pass by the trading post and leave literature. Geronimo remembers a Sunday School paper containing a picture of a Jewish Passover feast. This impressed him as a very young child. Later his parents sent him to the Methodist mission school in Farmington, where he received Bible teaching. The story of Daniel who prayed to God *three times a day* influenced his early life.

"I used to go behind a laundry building there at the mission school and pray, in the morning, at noon, and in the evening," he remembered.

Later, through the testimony of a fellow Navajo, he acknowledged Christ as Savior and was baptized. He finished high school at an Indian school in Albuquerque and soon thereafter determined to be a missionary to his own people. He worked for a number of years as an interpreter for Christian Reformed missionaries before meeting members of Wycliffe.

"The Lord has taught me many lessons through my physical blindness," says Geronimo. "I would say it has been a blessing to me."

Doubtless his need to learn to read Braille contributed to the patience and perseverance necessary for Bible translation.

Early in 1946 the revision of Mark was completed, and Dr. Nida suggested that Geronimo work ahead independently on a tentative translation of Matthew. Faye concentrated on the Pauline Epistles. Even with only part-time help from Geronimo—for he was still working with the

Christian Reformed mission as interpreter—Faye was making good progress. She expressed her delight with the collaboration of her Navajo partner:

"His keen mind was only made keener and his spiritual life deepened by his affliction. He was a strict teacher of his language. As I read back a translation he would detect even the faintest error in pronunciation—which reflected an error in spelling."

Heavy translation work required long hours of study, not only of Navajo grammar but of commentaries and Greek lexicons, as she dug out the original meanings of expressions in order to convert them into the language of The People. It was a difficult challenge, but Faye loved it.

Occasionally she would take time from her heavy translation schedule to teach reading to Navajos wanting to become literate. There was a new government movement afoot in Indian education, sparked by linguists and anthropologists who were seriously and sympathetically studying the Navajo situation. A new alphabet, based upon scientific studies, was now being used by the specialists working under the Bureau of Indian Affairs. Faye was asked to cooperate in the preparation of materials to be used in bilingual schools.

At times she was torn between two great tasks—translation for the people and literacy of the people. She was tempted to frustration, for she recognized her lack of time and specific preparation for the latter. But what good would a translated Bible be if the Navajos could not read it?

At the Methodist school Faye had met Faith Hill, a schoolteacher from California who was pinch-hitting as assistant matron for young Indian boys. With a strong interest in the Navajo people, she had spent her summer vacations as well as occasional years of leave of absence to work on the reservation. She had earned her Master's degree at Whittier College, California, with a thesis entitled *Education for*

Navajos: Problems Involved in Working out a Plan of Education for Navajo Indians. The substance for the thesis had grown out of firsthand pioneer experience in unschooled, isolated Navajo areas. She had also written a charming story of a Navajo boy, *Ashkee of Sunshine Water,* which had been published by Row, Peterson and Company in 1941. Her providential preparation for Navajo literacy was eloquently self-evident.

Faith had long wished that she could spend her whole life with the Navajos, but responsibility for her eighty-year-old mother was a deterrent. The Hills were practicing Quakers who believed strongly in the quiet leading of the Holy Spirit. When Mrs. Hill discerned her daughter's deep desire to live with the Navajos, she said to her one day, in the intimate Quakerese dialect, "I will go with thee."

So the plucky little octogenarian had packed up with her daughter, and the two of them were all set for a move to the Navajos. Feeling her need for instruction in the Navajo language, Faith had followed clues which would lead to the location of "a Miss Faye Edgerton" who was "specializing" in Navajo study. One of Faith's missionary friends had written to her about Faye's work and location.

"I had never met Faye, because she was over on the eastern part of the reservation. I had always worked on the western side. But I had heard that Miss Edgerton, of all the missionaries, had really worked on the language."

Faith wrote inquiring about the possibility of living near Faye in order to profit from her knowledge of the language.

"Faye wrote back saying that would be fine," Faith recollected, "but she had no idea where she was going to be! When she found out she would let me know. Mother and I waited all summer. We were all packed, ready to go—but we didn't know where we were going. Finally we received a card from Faye saying that she had decided on Farmington. So then we looked up Farmington on the map and found out where we were going!"

Temporary work at the Methodist mission school provided living quarters for the Blounts and for Faith and her mother. The Blounts later decided to build a home at the corner of Auburn and Animas streets in Farmington. At last the team was assembled under one roof. Faith, her mother, and Faye accepted the invitation to live at the Blounts' "hogan." Conveniently located on a street which led to a local trading post, it was right on the town "trail" of Navajos. They were made welcome and often dropped in for a chat.

The Wycliffe hogan was a hive of activity. It hummed with language-related projects from early in the morning until very late at night. Two schedules were in full force: producing the Scriptures in Navajo and producing educational materials which would help The People learn to read them. Faith Hill was working on professional literacy charts and primers, illustrated by Helen Blount's artistic drawings. Turner was busy with trips to hogans and schools where Navajos were beginning to show interest in reading their language.

Faye and Geronimo worked long hours on translation. He had been released from other responsibilities and was now translating full time. But the room in which they spent their days resembled a ward in a home for the handicapped more than a translator's study. For by this time Faye's remote and recent labors, under rugged conditions, had begun to take a cumulative toll on her body. She had developed a case of pernicious anemia and had been ordered to bed by the doctor. She could not put her feet to the floor without severe dizziness, and she was forced to work in bed.

"Of course, it didn't make any difference to Geronimo," Faye chuckled. Her bed was hardly visible, for it was cov-

ered with Bibles and books—commentaries and lexicons—
and papers, a sea of papers surrounding a small translator.

Geronimo sat beside her, "reading" with his hands, as
they worked all day, day aft, r day, on the translation.

At times when Faye was forced to rest, Geronimo would
press ahead on the translation of Matthew—but he needed
a scribe. Faith Hill was delighted to be his secretary as he
dictated the translation, for this was an excellent means of
studying the language.

Faith's functions were not confined to linguistics and literacy, however.

Tirelessly active and of a perpetually happy spirit, Faith
lubricated the wheels of the busy translation-literacy center.
She was a truly biblical peacemaker. There were times of
tension in the heavy schedule when this quality was of the
essence.

"You just can't *pick* a fight with Faith!" Faye said, marveling at her disposition. "She is completely unselfish. She
always freed me from household duties so I could translate,"
she added. "She *spoiled* me—just as my father had spoiled
me when I was young!"

"I am blessed of God in having the help of Miss Faith
Hill," she once wrote.

Mother Hill, in delicate health, was often confined to
bed. Although she was another patient in Faith's home-
hospital, she helped by praying for the important activities
going on around her. With strong faith in God and deep
appreciation for the many extra steps occasioned by the bed-
ridden household, she would often say quietly to her
daughter, "I am praying for thee."

God answered her prayers abundantly as first a trickle,
then a broadening stream, of Navajo literature began to
issue from the busy home. Many pages of manuscript which
went typed to the printer, had been tapped out painstakingly by Faith. She had mastered the Navajo script on her

"The Homestead" in Hastings, Nebraska, where Faye Edgerton was born on March 26, 1889.

Faye, a mischievous child at school, enjoyed the attention of a doting father and the guidance of a wise mother. She is shown here at age eight.

"Fedgie" at fifteen majored in fun yet always maintained high grades in school.

High school graduation in 1907 found "Fedgie" undecided as to her purpose in life.

After spending ten years first as a piano teacher and later as a missionary candidate at Moody Bible Institute, a committed Faye Edgerton served in Korea under the Presbyterian Mission Board. She posed in 1922 with her "Korean family," who helped her master their language.

Cornfields Community Center on the Navajo reservation near Granado, Arizona. Faye, shown here in 1924 with her Indian companion, was to pioneer in Indian education and social work that would span many years and result in the translation of the Navajo New Testament.

A joint conference of Navajo Christian leaders and Wycliffe Bible Translators was called in 1950 by the American Bible Society, represented by Henry Waterman (at blackboard) and Eugene Nida (far right). Its purpose was to make decisions concerning terms to be used in the Navajo New Testament. Faye Edgerton (seated before blackboard) listens to the discussion. The translation was completed in 1954 and published in 1956 under the title *God Bizaad*, God's Word.

God Bizaad motivated The People, as the Navajos call themselves, to learn to read in order to "hear" God speaking. In this scene a Navajo hogan in Rough Rock, Arizona, becomes a classroom when visited by Mary Gafford, a Friends Mission teacher. (*Paul Smith Photo*)

A mission schoolroom in Cortez, Colorado, where Warren Davis teaches from the Navajo New Testament. (*Paul Smith Photo*)

On to Apache country and another language. In San Carlos, Arizona, Faye Edgerton and Faith Hill occupied the compact 12′ x 14′ cabin at right as they translated the Apache New Testament. This task, begun in 1955, was completed in 1965.

Inside the cabin, Apache Christians confer with Faye and Faith on the final text.

September 25 has been declared by Congress as Bible Translation Day. It was first observed in 1966, shortly after the timely publication of the Apache New Testament. Faye Edgerton and Britton Goode, Apache representative, appear as speakers during the inaugural ceremony held at the Senate building.

Following the Bible Translation Day ceremony, a copy of the Apache New Testament was presented to President Lyndon B. Johnson. Cameron Townsend, General Director of the Wycliffe Bible Translators, and Mrs. Britton Goode look on as Mr. Goode reads a passage to The Hon. Mike N. Mantos, Administrative Assistant to the President, who will accept the book on behalf of President Johnson. (*Cornell Capa* © *Magnum Photos*)

Faye Edgerton consulted many versions of the Bible. Paul Smith captures her in a candid shot as she happily prepares for a study session with fellow translators.

typewriter with a special keyboard; the pages were perfect, typed with care.

Many times, long after her patients were safely tucked in for the night and the dishes all washed, Faith was happily at the typewriter, peck-peck-pecking away into the small hours, thankful to be a member of the exciting team.

12

Talking Sticks and Talking Paper

BEFORE MANY MOONS had passed it became apparent that there was too much activity at the corner of Auburn and Animas to be contained in one ordinary house. Soon Faye and Faith were building a companion home next to the Blounts. Navajos had discovered the corner where they were always welcome, and the houses were seldom without visitors. Overnight quarters were also constructed where out-of-town friends could enjoy Christian hospitality.

In 1947 another able assistant, Miss Anita Wencker, joined the team to help Faith in the increasing opportunities for teaching adults to read. She also proved to be a gifted hostess who made visiting Navajos feel at home. Faye said of her: "She had a lovely, gracious way with her, a deliberate way that the Navajos liked. They loved her very much."

Anita was also a companion for Mrs. Hill when it was necessary for Faith to be away teaching classes on the reservation. Even after Faye had regained her health enough to be up and around, her main task was to keep at the translation desk with Geronimo, many long hours each day. She had less and less time to sit and chat sociably with either Navajos or housemates.

As Faith continued to develop literacy books and aids, the home gradually took on the air of a schoolhouse.

"Our living room walls were covered with reading charts, and few who came got away without a lesson!" laughed Faye, remembering the educational fervor of her partners. They would rather teach than eat any time!

One visitor who came quite frequently was Old Mary, a medicine woman who lived on the mesa overlooking Farmington. She and her daughters would sometimes stay overnight at the translators' home, knowing that they would receive a full exposure to the sacred Scriptures and the secular alphabet. Faith was hopeful that Old Mary was believing what she heard of the Word of God, but Faye was skeptical. She had particular misgivings about her efforts to learn to read.

"She didn't stick at it enough to really learn," Faye commented. She felt that Old Mary's attempt to read was a "publicity stunt," to impress her own people.

Old Mary was notorious for the ceremonies which she carried on in her hogan. They attracted Navajos for miles around. Her specialty was the ability to "make the prayer sticks talk." Inside her hogan around the back wall she placed carved sticks, decorated with feathers, in the ground. When the ceremony was about to begin, she would order the people to sit facing the sticks. She sat in the back of the hogan. People would ask questions, and the sticks would "answer."

Faye recounted the opinion of one Navajo concerning the sticks: "He told us that he didn't believe that those sticks talked. One time he sat at the side of the hogan where he could watch Old Mary. He said that he couldn't see her lips move at all, but whenever those spirits who were supposed to be talking through the sticks would pause, or take a breath, he could see her take a breath. He believed that she did it somehow—he didn't quite know how."

And then Faye added: "She had learned to throw her voice, perhaps by ventriloquism, so that it sounded as though it came from the sticks. She was pretty clever, I tell you! It gave her a lot of prestige and power."

Although Old Mary's daughters showed sincere interest in the gospel and in reading, she herself went from bad to worse. When the oil companies came in she leased some of her land to them. With the money she bought cars, although she could not drive. Then she married a young husband and began to drink quite heavily. They would both come into town and get drunk. She would become very angry because her husband was so drunk he couldn't drive them home—and she didn't know how!

"He wouldn't do what she wanted," Faye said in conclusion. "Old Mary had a hard time with her young husband."

Government literacy efforts on the reservation were begun during World War II under the direction of Robert Young and William Morgan, experts in the Navajo language, who developed practical lessons for Indians needing to know English. These educators used the Indian language as a means of teaching English, by preparing bilingual textbooks. They used an alphabet based on symbols or written units known to linguists as phonemes. The phonemic Navajo alphabet was more satisfactory than previous ones, for it recognized the significance of long vowels and tones in the language. The linguists printed a monthly bilingual newspaper and published pamphlets on grazing regulations, the laws covering the use of agricultural land, and other information pertinent to tribal living. These were issued so

Navajos might understand "what the cop wants them for." one government educator explained. Birth certificates and other documents were also issued in diglot versions.

The Wycliffe ·Navajo team collaborated in this government literacy movement. Even after the war years the translators' cooperation with the program continued, with very cordial relations.

Robert Young was sympathetic with efforts to use Navajo in activities involving the tribespeople. In a letter to Faye, he wrote: "I am happy that you are carrying on the work of teaching literacy. I want to cooperate and collaborate with every person on the reservation who is concerned with or interested in Navajo literacy. By working together we can accomplish wonders; disunited our individual efforts are puny."

And cooperate he did! The translators provided him with the substance of lessons and charts. These were printed by government facilities and are still in use, in revised form, on the reservation.

Under the supervision of Young, with the help of John P. Harrington and Oliver La Farge, Indian education began to advance rapidly among The People. One of the chief factors responsible for the change was the reactivation of the Navajo Tribal Council, which began to shoulder responsibility for self-government. Up to that time the body had been only a symbol, an inactive group of Navajo leaders. Now decisions concerning The People were placed in their hands.

Teaching adults to read was a specialty which required skill and patience, but Faith and her team were rewarded by highly successful classes in a number of places on the reservation.

Turner spent considerable time in individual hogans and

at mission stations conducting reading classes. At a Nazarene mission at Ramah, New Mexico, he lived for several weeks while teaching an accelerated course. He roomed next to some of the Navajo pupils, and each morning he awoke to the tune of "ba, be, bi, bo; na, ne, ni, no," as his pupils chanted the syllables of the chart under attention. By intensive instruction, some of these earnest pupils were able to read a simplified version of the creation story at the end of two weeks. They were busy adults and were eager to learn to read God's Word as soon as possible.

Among the serious students was a Navajo storekeeper who managed the local cooperative. When he read that God had set apart one day of the week for rest, he closed the store on Sunday and came to church. An anthropologist working in the area found the store closed and came to the church, asking the storekeeper to open it. The Navajo replied firmly, "No. We have been reading that we are to worship God on Sunday, and I'm not going to open the store."

Another determined student was Sheppy Martine, an ex-medicine man who had been converted and wanted with all his heart to learn to read. Sheppy and his brother arrived at the school after all accommodations had been taken, and there was no place for them and their families to live. A short distance from the mission they discovered a *ch'iindi*, a haunted hogan in which a person had died and which a Navajo would ordinarily not even approach. To the horror of onlookers, Sheppy's brother tore the hogan down, loaded the logs into a pickup truck, returned to the mission, and set up a dwelling for the shelterless families.

Sheppy had declared to friends who urged him to return to his former trade as medicine man, "Never! Now I have a greater power, the power of God's Word. Why should I return?" So eager was he to read that he had fasted and prayed two days and two nights, beseeching God's help in the literacy venture. He knew no English and was completely unschooled; this was the opportunity of a lifetime.

God answered his petition. Sheppy not only learned to read, but he later became the faithful pastor of a group of believers in a remote area where he is still powerfully proclaiming the Word of God.

13

"What's Money?"

FAYE THOROUGHLY ENJOYED talking with Navajos who dropped in to visit. As often as she could afford the luxury, she would take time out of the strenuous translation schedule she had set for herself, just to chat with visitors.

One day a young Navajo who knew very little English appeared at the door. Faye, who happened to be "receptionist," found that he was from an area called Bistai, about forty miles south of Farmington. He had heard about the white women who knew Navajo and wanted to greet them. Although uneducated, he was curious about the "papers" they were writing.

"He kept glancing up at the charts which covered our walls," Faye remembered. "I asked him if he could read Navajo."

"Yes—a little," was his answer.

"I was skeptical," Faye continued, "but I got out our primers. I showed him the first one—and he zipped right through it! Then I showed him the second, and he read that quickly. Then the third—and by that time I was bug-eyed! I thought I would see if he could *really* read, so I got out the Navajo newspaper published by the government—and he read it."

"Where did you learn to read Navajo?" Faye asked, astonished at his ability.

The young man, Roger Deal, explained that he had been in a tuberculosis sanatorium. He and a fellow patient had procured a copy of the Navajo-English dictionary prepared by Robert Young under the Bureau of Indian Affairs. They had studied Navajo from the dictionary, their only textbook. They had taught themselves to read Navajo and had become so enthusiastic that they formed a class. They followed a regular schedule of classes every morning and every afternoon. Roger and his friend were the teachers.

"Before Roger came to visit us we had received letters from that hospital in Fort Defiance," Faye continued. "They were written in beautiful Navajo, requesting literature in the native language. We could not imagine how the patients had learned to read, for we knew no one there who was teaching reading. I showed Roger the letters."

"Oh, yes," he said. "Those are from my friends"—friends whom Roger had taught.

In the hospital he had been very ill and thought he was going to die. At that time he said that he had prayed to "the missionaries' God."

"What did you ask Him when you prayed to Him?" Faye queried, thinking that perhaps he had simply asked to be cured.

"Well, I asked Him that I might live in heaven forever," Roger responded.

In the following days, as they became well acquainted, Faye heard his story:

> My father is a medicine man. When I was a child he was always praying to the spirits, sometimes in our home and sometimes outdoors. Sometimes he went to

the hills to pray. Very early in the morning he prayed, sprinkling white cornmeal toward the rising sun. At noon he sprinkled corn pollen upward toward the sun, and at evening he sprinkled yellow cornmeal toward the setting sun.

My grandmother lived with us and she prayed a lot too. She always prayed after we ate. Her prayers, and my father's too, were that they might be well and strong, have lots of food, and many sheep and horses. There were six of us children, but we never learned any prayers. In the evening we threw corn pollen toward the west, like everyone else did. We didn't know why, except that if we did we would be lucky and happy.

Our family hogan was made of stone. The roof was of logs skillfully fitted together without any upright poles to hold it up. Most hogans are made of logs and do not have any windows, but ours had windows. The floor was of flat stones covered with mud like cement. It had a covering of goat and cattle skins sewed together. In the middle of the hogan under a hole purposely left for the smoke in the roof, the fire burned. There was a vein of coal about three miles from our home, so that was our fuel. It was always warm in our hogan, even on the coldest nights.

In the evenings as we sat around the fire, my grandmother would tell us stories of how people came to be on the earth, and of how and where the sun was made, and where the sheep and horses came from. She told of the crafty coyote who was always playing tricks on the other animals and on people. She told of the giants who lived on the earth. Sometimes she told stories of the Giant Killer, the son of Changing Woman. These stories were only told in the winter from the time of the first frost until spring. There were other stories about the bear which could only be told in the winter while he slept.

When I was about six years old I began to herd the sheep with an uncle and a cousin. We often left before dawn and followed the sheep till sunset. We took some corn or some tortilla in our pockets for our lunch, but we often killed a rabbit or prairie dog with a sling-shot or bow and arrow. Then we would broil the game over the coals of fire we had made. Later my cousin and uncle both went to school but my father said I must take care of the sheep, although I wanted very much to go to school.

Sometimes I went with my father and the other men and boys to the medicine men's ceremonies. In the summer we went to the squaw dances and in the winter to the *yeibichai*. I thought I was having a good time going around to these ceremonies and to the movies in town.

During all those years I heard the gospel just a little from a Navajo Christian who was also a member of the Tribal Council. He came to our home to discuss other things, but he also told the gospel to my people. I heard only a little, however, because I was always busy herding the sheep. I did not understand it and I did not think about it.

When I was nineteen I went to work at a government ammunition storage place about eighty miles from my home.

When I was twenty-one my father picked out a wife for me. We gave her mother five horses, some jewelry, and some sheep. We had a Navajo ceremony at her home at night, and then in the morning the missionary came and married us in the white man's way. I went to live at my wife's home, as is the custom of my people. There I helped my wife's family by hauling water and wood and sometimes herding sheep.

Most of the time, though, I was away working on the railroad with other Navajos.

Once I went to San Francisco to work in the ship-yards. A white man who worked beside me coughed a lot, and sometimes spit blood. From him I got tuber-culosis, but I didn't know what I had. I got very thin, but I kept on working until finally I was too sick to go back to work.

I went back to my father's home, and he called in his uncle and other medicine men to sing over me. They sang and prayed over me many times, but I was never healed. I spit blood a lot and was often un-conscious.

The missionaries who lived not far away came fre-quently to our home and told us about the Lord Jesus. I remember the story of the prodigal son, and of the Good Shepherd especially, but I didn't understand very well.

Finally the missionaries asked my father if they could take me to the hospital. He consented, but the sana-torium was full, so they took me to their home and cared for me there for a week or so until they could take me to the hospital. Their interpreter talked to me every day about the Lord, and I was thinking about what they said.

At the hospital a Navajo Christian worker who came to visit often talked to me about the gospel, and I heard Christian radio messages too. They told me I should get rid of my sin by asking God to forgive me, and by accepting His Son Jesus into my heart. I thought about what they said very much.

For a while I got better, then I got worse and almost died. I began to pray to the missionaries' God. I asked that I might get well, but I also prayed that I might live in heaven forever with God. I think I was really saved at that time.

Roger was obviously hungry to know more of the Word of God. He was happy to be taught in Navajo, for he understood little English. Faye discovered, as her association with Roger continued, that he was an excellent person with whom to check translation. Unfamiliar with the English text, he was dependent upon the Navajo for understanding.

Soon an attic room at the translators' home was converted into living quarters for Roger, who began to help with the translation. Geronimo became his roommate as they cooperated in an all-out effort to complete the New Testament in their language.

"He was very helpful to us," Faye said. "If he didn't understand the sequence of events, or the reference of pronouns, he would speak up and say, 'Who did that?' or 'Who said that?' "

Geronimo, familiar with the contents of the Bible, would anticipate the action of the narrative under consideration, but it was a new Book to Roger.

During the winter of 1949 the two men worked happily on translation, although the pay they received was very small. The translators shared with them as generously as possible, but their own income was limited and expenses were multiple in the miniature school-home-translation center.

Roger had talked of looking for a job where he might earn some money, perhaps as a cook's helper in a railroad repair gang. He was not yet strong enough for hard physical labor.

As spring approached, Faye asked Roger one day, "Are you still planning to work with the railroad gang this summer?"

He was sitting at Faye's desk. Placing his hand on the Bible, he said, "No, I'm not going to do that. This is what I want my people to have, and I want to help get it ready for them."

"You won't make much money doing *that!*" Faye said with emphasis. "We can't pay you very much."

"What's *money?*" he said. "It won't last forever—but this Book will. I want my people to have it."

14

"At Any Cost . . ."

PATIENCE, prayer—and pains.

It was an old formula, one used by John Wycliffe in the translation of the first English Bible. And there had been no improvement upon it—at least as far as Faye could tell. Working with the living Word of God offered its own rich rewards. The labor itself was, in a sense, self-renewing to the laborer. But this work, though loved, brought "weariness to the bones."

Long hours of delving into commentaries and the thorough tracing out of theological arguments were necessary to satisfy the diligent Navajo collaborators who looked to Faye for answers.

For example, what should be done about the word for baptism? Various forms of baptism were used on the reservation, depending upon the interpretation of denominations working in different areas. Some sprinkled, some dipped—and some took the sacrament as verbal symbolism and did nothing. How then should this ritual, mentioned often in the New Testament, be translated?

To ascertain the convictions and reactions of Navajos and missionaries involved in these important decisions, it was necessary for Faye to drive many miles over the reservation in the Volkswagen. She enjoyed the opportunity to spend periods of time with her colleagues in the Navajo field extending over parts of Arizona, New Mexico, Colorado, and Utah.

Checking, checking, everlastingly checking.

Revising, changing, typing, consulting with fellow translators.

The schedule was stimulating but wearing. Early in 1950 Faye began to show signs of fatigue, and her companions were concerned about her. Faith and Anita—and Mrs. Hill when her health permitted—relieved her of many household chores and the receiving of Indian visitors. Thus Faye and her Navajo team could spend full days on the translation.

In 1949 several books of the New Testament had been published as separate portions: the Gospel of Matthew— Geronimo's special project—Philippians, James, First Peter, and First Corinthians. William Goudberg and Jacob Kamps of the Christian Reformed mission had collaborated on the Corinthian Epistle, giving valuable assistance in hammering out difficult theological concepts and expressing them in Navajo. In addition, a good remaining portion of the New Testament was either in first draft or in some stage of revision previous to publication. Progress on the monumental project, which at one time appeared to defy completion, was most gratifying.

As her prayer for the year, Faye wrote in her diary at the beginning of 1950:

Let me be a sherd, Lord, ready to Thy hand, to give the

Water of Life to the Navajos. Gideon's pitchers had to be broken before they gave out the light. Let me be a broken pitcher: let the light of Thy Word shine forth to the Navajos, at any cost.

On her sixty-first birthday, March 26 of the same year, she noted in her diary:

My birthday. Lord, my one desire is that Thou shalt indeed be all in all, that Thou shalt live and love and work through me, in Thy fullness, to the saving of souls and the strengthening of them in Thy Word. I renew, Lord, the pledge of these last pages of my life, and give myself to Thee anew for Thy desire.

Perhaps the strain of the previous months and years had prompted her to feel that the remaining pages of her life were numbered, for she seldom referred to her age as a deterrent in her task. But she was visibly worn and needed physical refreshing.

By summertime her co-workers persuaded her to change her pace and take time off for a trip to Utah with Turner Blount. He was to attend an Indian conference at Silver Forks near Salt Lake City and was pleased when Faye agreed to accompany him.

It was August—hot, oppressively hot, on the Utah plateau. The searing sun beat down in deadly determination on Turner's pickup truck as it sped along the desolate desert highway. It was no wonder that Faye had been droned into a deep sleep, her graying head thrown back in complete relaxation against the right-hand door of the cab. Turner was fighting drowsiness, but he was deliberately alert and eager to reach his destination.

Only a few more hours, he thought, as the pickup whined and vibrated over the burning highway.

Suddenly the truck lurched and bucked like a frightened deer. Before Turner knew what had happened, the vehicle was off the road, plowing through clouds of blinding dust, bouncing out of control over clods and clumps of desert grass. The right front tire had blown out.

"I struggled to apply the brakes," Turner recalled, "but bouncing over bunches of grass growing in little islands in the eroded sand caused my foot to vibrate so that I couldn't get the truck stopped for some time. Finally I ground to a halt in a storm of dust and sand.

"I jumped out on the driver's side and ran around to Faye, who had been thrown out. As we had gone over the rough shoulder of the road, the twisting of the pickup had caused the door to fly open. Faye had fallen head first, face up, but still caught in the door by both her feet. Somehow or other she had been wedged in and held firmly until we stopped.

"There she was, almost buried in dust and sand, her mouth and eyes open but filled with desert dirt. Of course I thought she was dead. I felt for her pulse, but there was none. There was no breathing.

"I flagged a car on the highway, and with a heavy heart I gathered up Faye's limp little body in my arms to take her to Price, the next town on the highway—about sixty long miles away.

"We put her in the back seat with her head on my lap," Turner continued. "As we sped toward Price we overtook a car with a waterbag hanging from the door. We hailed the car and borrowed the bag. I soaked some Kleenex in the water and dripped it drop by drop between Faye's teeth."

After a while Faye blinked and gasped. Regaining consciousness, she asked, "Where are we going?"

"We're going to Price," Turner said.

"I don't *want* to go to Price," Faye said with characteristic determination.

"Well, we've got to get you fixed up a little bit there," Turner answered.

"But I don't want to go to Price . . . I have no business there . . . I have *work* to do . . . ," Faye said, her words trailing as she lapsed again into unconsciousness.

Turner seriously doubted that she would ever finish that "work," and he was sick at heart. The Navajo team had depended upon Faye to carry the heavy end of the translation load.

Turner tried not to think. But the small body was so limp and lifeless. *What if Faye should not recover? How long would it take us to finish the Testament?*

The road seemed interminable.

"I tried to keep her quiet as we rolled along," Turner continued. "I saw that her right ear was almost completely torn from the side of her head. Her right arm was skinned from the wrist to the shoulder. I didn't know what other injuries she had suffered.

"By the time Faye was on the operating table in the hospital in Price she was quite rational. She told me to go on to the conference. In three days I could stop by and pick her up, and we would return to Farmington. I stayed around and talked to the doctor. He, too, told me to go on, since there was nothing I could do.

"But first I had to go back for the pickup truck and all our gear scattered across the desert. A newly made friend took me back to the dismal scene. There was the truck with the doors wide open, skid marks smeared across the highway and sand, and our personal belongings strewn everywhere. The suitcases had popped open in flight, throwing our clothes in every direction. Footprints covered the ground around the truck where people had stopped to look, but nothing was disturbed. No one had taken anything.

"I took a good look at the tracks, wondering how Faye could have stayed pinned by her feet to the truck for such a distance. At the right-hand side of the tracks, about every eight or nine feet there was a little depression in the soft sand. This is where her head hit as it bounced. Her head would hit, then bounce and swing for about nine feet, then drop, hit, and bounce to the next point. Only the Lord preserved her life. Any less hardy soul would have given up on the first bounce, I'm sure."

Turner went to the Indian conference and returned to Price in three days. He found that shortly after he had left, Faye had gone into shock. Two broken ribs were discovered, and she was badly bruised and shaken. She could not go with Turner now.

By the following week Faye had recovered sufficiently to fly to Farmington. Her partners welcomed her back but were concerned about her condition following such an accident.

"She didn't seem to have any serious aftereffects," Turner commented, marveling at her vitality. "She bounced back in short order. Her wounds healed up and she was soon ready for the *next* crisis . . ."

Crises, small and great, had punctuated Faye's sixty-one years. And though it seemed that she was accident prone, no crippling calamity had befallen her. Now, once again, she had been delivered from death by an unseen hand which had secured her feet in the door of the runaway truck and had cushioned the blows of her head on the desert turf.

Recuperating in the Price hospital, Faye had had time to reflect upon the events of the previous days, and of the years before.

I could have died several times, she thought. *But here I am, my life spared once more . . .*

Scenes from earlier days when her life had hung by a thread flashed through her mind. There was the almost fatal case of scarlet fever when she was a young girl. She might have died from a later severe case of pneumonia. She recalled the illnesses in Korea and the nervous breakdown.

The accident that had pinned her under her car in Flagstaff could have snuffed out her life.

Remembering with gratitude the recent escape from death on the desert, Faye wrote in her diary:

Aug. 8, 1950—Price, Utah. Thank you, Lord Jesus, for saving my life again a week ago on the way to Salt Lake City. I give it back to Thee and pray that Thou will fill me and use me as never before. Make every day, every moment, count for Thee.

15

Can God Speak Navajo?

"WE MUST CHANGE, of course. But *that which stands up in us* is Navajo; if we destroy it, life isn't worth living."

Myron thought hard. "But there are so few Indians. All the hair will be short soon, everyone will go to school."

"That doesn't matter. It isn't numbers or long hair or living in hogans. It's *that which stands up in you,* the same thing which makes one man by his voice and his eyes control many hundreds to go this way or that. Numbers can't destroy that. Life is full of pains and disappointments, yet life is worth living, so long as you have that."

Oliver La Farge*

As the translation trio forged ahead day by day, discussing and debating, probing and praying, the precious piles of paper grew higher. It was a tedious but rewarding task, not unlike the careful craftsmanship of a Navajo silversmith who sets out to make a beautiful turquoise and silver necklace or bracelet. He first conceives the design, then he

*Op. cit., p. 100.

painstakingly works until "in beauty it is finished." Finishing a verse "in beauty" required the thoughtful twisting and turning of words—and sometimes the heat of earnest argument!

In the process of transforming thoughts into another verbal mold, Faye was the bridge between two worlds, a link between two languages. The onus of explaining what the original text meant rested upon her. And often the manner of expressing the thought of a biblical concept in the Indian tongue was worlds away from either Greek or English!

How overjoyed were the Navajo teammates when after a struggle with ideas the words spoke clearly and the sense of a passage was rendered with a strong impact in their own language!

"Our minds are tied up," Roger would sometimes say with a sigh when the meaning had not yet emerged.

"Now my mind is resting," he would say when it was revised to his satisfaction.

Once he was overheard saying to a fellow Navajo: "This isn't just a missionary talking to us in another language— this is God's Word in Navajo. It is just like God talking! It is like a fire burning inside me."

Such reactions were high pay for a Bible translator.

When a book of the New Testament was completed, Faye would read it to other Navajos to test for intelligibility. She found that the people of the tribe were highly individualistic; what some approved others would reject, and further revision would often be needed. Missionaries of the entire denominational spectrum were consulted, and many graciously cooperated in the checking of The Book. Even those who had once doubted the necessity of its translation into Navajo became interested and facilitated the circulation of tentative drafts for review among Navajos in their associations.

Passages familiar to English readers but hitherto hidden from The People began to speak in vigorous, idiomatic phrases. The verses in Matthew 11 promising rest to the weary now said to them; "Those of you whose strength-put-forth is killing you, and whose loads are heavy, all of you come to me and I will cause you to rest. Like horses harnessed side by side, work with me and learn of me. I do not talk back, and I think of myself as lowly. Through learning of me, that which stands up in you will rest."

Frequently a picturesque Navajo phrase turned out to be the most apt equivalent of one word in the original. The concept of soul was expressed in Navajo by the expression "that which stands up in you." Other abstract terms, such as those for spirit and heart, were translated in various idiomatic ways. For example, "Let not your heart be troubled" became "Don't have many minds," and "that your joy may be full" was rendered "that you be happy to the complete capacity of your minds."

There were days when the two Indian men were happy to the "complete capacity" of their minds, when the turning of the thought into facile word patterns of their language was sheer joy. They loved the parables speaking of sheep. Then they were in home territory, for shepherding is a common occupation among Navajos, and terms concerning sheep are frequently used. Losing a lamb is a well-known experience on the reservation, where the eroded land has many pitfalls and treacherous canyons into which unguarded animals can fall. Even the parable of the wise man who built his house upon a rock was comparatively easy to translate. Flash floods and quicksand are familiar phenomena in Navajoland, and outcroppings of rock large enough to build a house upon are not uncommon.

Another Bibleland concept paralleled in Navajo thinking was that of silversmithing, one of the main industries of the tribe. The account of the silversmiths' riot in the book of Acts presented no difficulty. Silver turns out to be "metal which is white," and a silversmith is "one who pounds metal which is white"—a long phrase in English, but the most compact and exact Navajo equivalent.

Many incidents recorded in the Gospels, and many figures of the New Testament based upon the common Palestinian occupation of fishing, were difficult for Navajo translators. In addition to the fact that there are few bodies of water in the reservation, there is the further complication that Navajo culture includes a taboo on eating fish. Thus the entire matter of fishing—terms for the activity itself, and the purpose of it—were alien to The People.

In the Navajo language the verbal expression of a motion necessarily includes an element of the word specifying the *kind* or *shape* of object used in a given motion or action. Thus in the language there was no general word for "fishing," although foreigners had been observed engaging in this exotic activity. Fishing with a line and fishing with a net had to be distinguished. A fisherman using a line turned out to be "one who draws fish up out of (water) by means of a ropelike object." And a fisherman using a net was rendered as "one who draws fish up out of (water) by means of a flat, flexible object." When a distinction in the type of fishing employed did not need to be specified, fishing by means of "a ropelike object" was used, since it was more familiar to Navajos than the otherworldly net fishing.

There was another problem in fishing stories peculiar to the Navajo language but seldom faced by readers of the English Bible. Words for siblings, brothers and sisters, necessarily denote whether the sibling is younger or older. In the translation of the story of the fishermen brothers in Mark, the Navajo translation reads: "Simon and his-younger-brother Andrew (customarily) drew fish up out of (water) by means of a flat, flexible object."

In the story of Mary and Martha, which sister is the

older? The original language does not indicate a fact which must be specified in Navajo. The conclusion was that since Martha seemed to take the responsibility of the housework, she was probably the older of the two. The narrative then concerned "Mary and her-older-sister-Martha."

Navajo distinguishes between a man's son or daughter, and a woman's son or daughter, by the use of different terms for each of these kinship categories. What term should be used in the expression "daughter of Zion"? Is Zion a man or a woman? On the basis of Old Testament usage in which cities were referred to as feminine, it was decided to assign Zion to a feminine category. "Daughter of Zion" was treated as "Zion, her-daughter."

Terms for king and kingdom were lacking, but the tribal culture traditionally provides for headmen, leaders. The word for headman is derived from a verb meaning "to move the head from side to side as in making an oration." The headman needed to be a good orator, able to persuade the people to go to war or to follow him in important decisions. He had to influence people by moving his head. The modern word for ruler or boss—functioning as a king—grew out of the head-moving concept. But how would one say "the highest ruler"? Superlatives presented another problem. The expression used in the translation, very freely rendered into English, is "of those who move the head from side to side, this one is the greatest."

If the idea of a king was foreign, a word for his crown was even more remote. Navajos have never worn even the headdress usually associated with American Indians. In early times men wore a scarf or handkerchief tied around their heads, a custom which is still observed by the older men of the tribe. A common modern head-covering is the big Western cowboy hat. The word finally chosen to express a king's crown was "hat of the one who moves his head from side to side."

Words to express the concept of evil spirits presented problems. The casting out of evil spirits was not difficult, inasmuch as in religious ceremonies medicine men gave emetic herbs to onlookers and patients. The vomiting produced was to expel evil spirits. But terms for the spirits were debatable. The common word for evil spirit refers to the ghost or spirit of a dead person. Such a spirit was always malignant. At first a word was coined to mean only evil spirit, not necessarily a ghost, in order to bypass the idea of fear of ghosts common to Navajos. This was abandoned when later an old Christian man exclaimed, "So what! Such a spirit may be evil—but it does not affect *me!*"

Another type of problem arose, stemming from the spelling of words in Navajo. Because of a subtle difference in the meaning of words hinging *only* upon the length of a vowel, or the tone on which a syllable was spoken, words had to be read accurately to convey exact meanings. Sometimes the mistake would stir up real trouble. The words for "altar" and "counter (upon which something is sold)" fell into this category. An altar, "that on which something is offered," is *náá'iiniihii;* the word for counter is *na'iiniihii,* "that on which trading is done." The only difference is in the length of the vowel in the first syllable, indicated by writing two vowels, and high tone, indicated by the acute accent mark. In rapid reading, these slight differences can easily be omitted in pronunciation.

On one occasion this mistaken pronunciation provoked a highly emotional discussion. The Navajo word for "one who trades something" was closely associated with the word for a counter in the trading post, and it conjured up to the Navajo the sheep reduction program that had been carried on only a few years before. Government stockmen had determined that the range on the Navajo reservation was seriously overgrazed, and they consequently ordered the Indians to trade their sheep in large numbers to the government at the counter in trading posts in order to reduce the grazing units. This was done at great personal cost to the Navajos, and with misunderstandings and frustrations. A very deep seated hatred for that project and all white men involved in it developed.

When a passage in Matthew referring to altar was read, The People confused it with the odious counter in the trading post.

When read carefully and correctly, the similar words presented no problem. The incident pointed up the need for thorough teaching of literacy, and attention to all the written symbols of Navajo.

Other problems were often easily solved by the simple addition of a syllable or component part of a word in Navajo which connoted a necessary distinction. For example, the word virgin was at first misunderstood. In Navajo there is a term which means "young woman of marriageable age," but in some cases it means simply "young woman." As an attempt to clarify the term, the words "one who does not have a husband" were added. When this expression concerning the virgin Mary in Luke was read, one person laughed and said, "That could mean that her husband had gone somewhere, or that her husband was dead!"

In the end Mary said, in Navajo, "I have no husband *yet.*"

Anxiety or care is expressed in Navajo by a word indicating that which prickles and irritates, like a pin sticking into the flesh. First Peter 5:7, which in English admonishes the believer to cast his care on the Lord, in Navajo says, "The things that are continually sticking into you, turn them over to me, for I am interested in you, and caring about you."

The words in First Thessalonians 5:21 which caution against false teaching, and encourage Christians to "test" or "try" such instruction, turn out in Navajo to say, "Track out all kinds of teaching"—like tracking a horse, or thief, until he is found.

Surprises sometimes lay hidden in an apparently innocent passage, where the translators would not have expected difficulty. One such instance was the expression for "Aaron's rod that budded," referred to in the Book of Hebrews. The informant wanted to know what kind of a tree the "rod" came from. When he was told that it was an almond tree, he wanted to know what *color* almond blossoms were. The color of the blossom is incorporated in Navajo terms for bud. There are many words for bud, depending on the color. The Navajo translation helper could not even *say* the word for bud without knowing the color the blossom would be!

When the members of the team reached the Book of Revelation they were ecstatic with the prospect of finishing The Book—but this last portion of the New Testament took considerable research. A number of musical instruments mentioned are not native to the Indian culture. Navajos are familiar only with the drum and a kind of flute called the *dilni*. In the holy concert mentioned in Revelation 18, pipers became "those who whistled through *dilni*," trumpeters "played the brass *dilni*," and harpers played "the wood that sings."

Words could always be found which would rejoice "that which stands up" in the Navajo, even if the research for these words was often long and sometimes exhausting—especially to a non-Navajo like Faye. But she persisted until the gems, the precious treasures in the beautiful language of The People, were mined and polished.

God did speak Navajo—and not with a foreign Palestinian accent or even in the twang of white man's America. He spoke in the warm, homespun vernacular of *Diné*, the shrine of The People's soul:

In the rhythm of the song of the Indian boy as he galloped on his spirited pony across the dusty Arizona desert . . .

In the sweet familiar intonation of the hogan, mingled with secure fragrance of smoke and sheepskins . . .

In the singing of the silversmith as he pounded and persuaded the shining white metal . . .

God spoke powerfully in the language of The People, and
He spoke in beauty.

16

Navajo Best Seller

THE NAVAJO LANGUAGE has a penchant for binary classification
of events or objects. They are viewed as being either *tangible*
or *intangible*. A time of need, or set of untoward circum-
stances, is expressed as "intangible things stretching along
beyond us."

For years the completion of the New Testament had been
something of a mirage, an intangible goal stretching on and
on, eluding termination. Like Everest, it was "always there."
But, unlike Everest, it was *intangible*—at least until the
manuscript could be terminally typed, bundled up, and sent
off to the American Bible Society for printing.

In 1952 the translators prepared for the final assault on
the summit, but the last ascent was arduous. A meeting of
Navajo leaders, missionaries, and Bible Society representatives was held to decide on final terms to be used in certain
trouble spots in the Testament. Much prayer had preceded
this gathering, for there were sensitive points to be considered. But the Wycliffe translators who had worked on
The Book were anxious that it be accepted and used by
all The People. They did not want a museum piece or an
item of acquisition for linguistic libraries: they wanted the

volume to be read, used, and applied to daily living. If certain groups were offended or alienated by terms used, The Book might not have ready acceptance.

Faye expressed gratitude to God for the harmony which prevailed in the 1952 meeting and for the spirit of unity among Navajos and missionaries as final decisions were made and the die cast.

On a serene September evening in Farmington in 1954, the quiet conquerors of the Navajo Everest found it difficult to suppress tears of joy. The precious manuscript was *finished!* The bundle of paper held many interlinear secrets, a lifetime of toil and triumph which could never be verbalized. But the package which soon went flying through the air to New York contained wealth more lasting than the recently discovered oil and uranium on the reservation. This was the wealth of a Word that would outlast everything on earth, as Roger had said.

During the following year, as "yards and yards of galley proof" were read and corrected, as all the Navajo jots and tittles were checked and double-checked, there were nights when the lights burned long at the corner of Auburn and Animas. But these were nights of almost sheer joy, an exhilarating weariness, in anticipation of the day fast approaching when The Book would be in the hands of The People.

As the team continued literacy work and the unceasing production of other literature in the Navajo language, overarching all was the constant question: Will the New Testament be *used?* Will The People want to read God's Word in their language? Some Anglos were still skeptical about the future use of the language, and about Bible translation in particular.

The translators had gone out on a limb. They had gambled —with confidence in God—on the strong possibility of its acceptance.

But how could one know, really, until The Book was off the press?

It was an unbearably hot August day in Norman, Oklahoma. Faye and Faith and the Blounts were on the 1956 staff of the Summer Institute of Linguistics under the direction of Dr. Kenneth Pike, who had given them their initial push into translating the Navajo New Testament.

Staff and students were weary, and some were tempted to discouragement as the heavy summer's work was nearing its end. The mounting pressure of final examinations, papers, and departure threatened to rob the final chapel gathering of a spirit of relaxed worship. Even the hour was unpropitious—soon after lunch, and in a gymnasium without air conditioning.

Faye went to her mailbox shortly before the afternoon meeting, and to her unbelieving eyes, there was a package airmailed from New York. It was the first copy of the Navajo New Testament.

Her ecstatic joy was shared immediately with Dr. Pike— who turned the unpromising chapel hour into a time of unrestrained praise to God. The spirit of thanksgiving was contagious, as students who had been struggling all summer to master difficult sounds and linguistic principles, preparatory to going out to the ends of the earth to translate the Bible, saw tangible proof that it *could be done*. Faye stood in humble gratitude before the group, giving God *"all* the glory" for the accomplishment. A fervent prayer for God's blessing upon the distribution and use of The Book closed the moving chapel service.

"Several of those going out soon to commence the task in a tribal language spoke of the encouragement it brought to their hearts," Faye wrote. "We felt it very gracious of the Lord to so perfectly time the arrival of the first copy."

"It looks so nice," Faye mused as she held the volume with

understandable affection. "A stiff black cover with a gold title in Navajo, red edges, nicely printed with clear type . . ." It was indeed a handsome volume.

Back in Farmington in September the main dedication service was held in the Navajo Christian Reformed Church. This was a gathering of The People, in their own land, to· receive their Book. Mr. Richard West, Denver representative of the American Bible Society, presented a copy to Geronimo, symbolically for the whole tribe. The blind translator "felt" the beauty of the book and shared the high moment of joy as he visualized the happy audience of Navajos who crowded out the church building and filled the surrounding lawn. In addition to the Wycliffe members of the team, there were Navajos who had faithfully and sacrificially helped in checking the manuscript: Mr. and Mrs. John Charles of Shiprock, Mr. Chee Anderson, Mr. Tom Dennison, and Miss Fannie Scott. These had longed for the day when the New Testament would be in the hands of their people, and they had worked to make this day a reality.

The ceremony was reported in the Farmington *Daily Times* as "an outstanding occasion for the tribe":

For the first time ever, the complete New Testament in the language of 80,000 Navajos was presented in public ceremonies. The publication has long been awaited, as the language was first reduced to writing in 1905 and the first portion of the Bible was printed in 1910.

A description of the place of dedication and of the Indian people in attendance was a commentary on the changing context in which the Scriptures would be used:

The Chapel, scrubbed and cleaned to perfection, expressed the modernization of the tribe. The tile floor, blond finished piano, knotty-pine paneled walls and overhead ceiling beams, along with steel screened windows and thermostat heating control, make this church not only comfortable, but tend to give atmosphere for sacred services.

The Navajos themselves, some dressed in tribal apparel and others in modern day dress, listened quietly and reverently to the ceremony being conducted in both English and Navajo.

Burr-haircuts were most prevalent. Navajo men and children were attired in jeans, T-shirts, and other up-to-date clothes.

The report stated that Mr. Anderson, the Navajo leader of the meeting, "touched the hearts of the entire congregation, Anglo and Indian alike, as he spoke in his native Navajo tongue, while caressing the New Testament. Then, holding it forth, he needed no translator to explain the meaning it held for his people."

In conclusion the account said, "Thus another big step has been taken in the history of the Navajo people."

Happy as the translators were, they knew that the real test would come in the following days as the Testament was put "on the market" on the reservation. Would The People desire it enough to pay seventy-five cents for it? Even though the low price was made possible by a subsidy through the Bible Society, it was more than some low-income families could afford.

Word of The Book's arrival spread quickly, as if a re-layed drumbeat announced its coming. The People were ready to buy. They had been waiting for it, for the Good News in printed form. They bought it immediately, and gladly.

The first edition of 2,500 volumes was sold out in five months—and a second edition of 2,000 was on the press. It also sold out rapidly, and a third edition was exhausted just as quickly as the previous printings.

The translators could hardly believe it themselves. This is what they had hoped for; this was their dream. But the reality was deeply gratifying. The Navajo people did not have the reading habit, for literature in their language was still scarce. Some had had little or no education, and reading at first was slow and laborious.

But The People loved their Book, and they learned to read it. Educated and uneducated alike seemed to hunger and thirst for words in their language which spoke of intangible but eternal reality.

Almost immediately every mission station instituted classes for reading the Navajo New Testament. Many had been using English versions, but the demand for the Scriptures in an intelligible version was so great that Navajo reading became the order of the day.

In one of the missions a bright young Indian girl learned to read Navajo in a couple of days. The next day she came to her teacher and said enthusiastically, "Do you know what I did last night? I lay on the ground by the fire and read the New Testament nearly all night—I just couldn't put it down!"

One person who had studied several years in a Bible school said, "It used to be all blurred and dark to me when I read it in English, but now it is as clear as light, because I understand it."

People who had never comprehended much more than the narratives of the Gospels were surprised at the teachings of the Epistles. One woman said, "I used to think I was a pretty good Christian, but now that I've read what God really expects of me, I see that I'm not."

Navajo pastors began to use the Testament in their preaching. It became the only textbook of preachers like Sheppy Martine who lacked education and thus needed the Word of God in their language as prime source material for sermons.

One pastor, after reading a chapter from First Corinthians to his congregation, said, "This is so clear in our language that I really don't have to preach a sermon now!"

Even those who had served as interpreters for missionaries were surprised at the contents of the New Testament when they read it for themselves in a language which spoke directly to them. In the final days of checking, before the book went to press, this reaction was observed. One well-educated Navajo had said, "I never understood the Bible before. I've learned a lot here at the translation desk."

Another who had taught the Bible in English for a number of years would exclaim as he studied the Navajo text, "Is *that* in the Bible? This is like a seminary course for me!"

Although it became a new book for those who had already studied in English, it became literally the book of life for those who had never gone to school. There was now strong motivation for learning to read, and many struggled for literacy in order to read the Word of God.

One Navajo took his Testament to work, to read in his spare moments. A companion noticed the book and asked about it. When the owner of the Testament proudly read to him from it, the friend wanted to own one. The owner gladly gave his own copy to his friend—and proceeded to buy himself another!

The People were not only buying—they were reading their Book. One Navajo wrote the translators: "The New Testament is winning many hearts, and is really a treasury to our people."

Comments from mission leaders said, "Our workers are holding several weekly reading classes with groups of people in hogans, and here at the mission."

"At our mission every new believer is expected to make an honest effort to read the Navajo New Testament."

It became the thing to do; using the Navajo Testament became the goal of missionaries who had previously used only English, for now the Navajo people themselves wanted the Bible in their language.

For some adults, learning to read was a heroic struggle. It required patience and persistence on the part of teacher and pupil.

Faith and Anita were busier than ever, day and night, teaching adults to read. Some could learn fairly quickly— but others were slow.

Ann was one who was very slow. Her mental processes had been retarded by the long use of peyote. A missionary had patiently worked with her, leading her to a knowledge of Christ. She became eager to read His Word, and with Anita's steadfast help when progress was almost impercept- ible, Ann finally learned to read. She became addicted to the reading of the Word of God! She wore out several copies by her constant reading. In recounting her experience she said:

I used to follow the old Navajo ways, and I ate peyote, but I never found any help for my troubles. Then one day a missionary said to me, "Come, let's go to the house of prayer and listen to God's Word."

So I did that. I listened to God's Word. I found out that God made the world and everything in it. He made *me!* So I thought, Why should I worship the things He made? They can't save me!

Thinking that way, I got a paper sack and put into it it all the things that used to be precious to me: the bit of pollen, the blue stones—and I thought, These are not holy.

Then I went to where the water is flowing. There I threw in all those things. I threw in the peyote, too, for I thought, This is not good. When one eats it, one's body gets weak.

After I had thrown them all into the water I was very happy about having done it. For God's Word in one place says, "You must not worship things that are made by hands. Worship me only. Then I will cause you to live eternally."

In another place His Word says, "Heaven and earth shall pass away, but my Word shall not pass away."

These things will all pass away, I thought, as I threw them into the water. They are just made-things. They are not to be worshiped.

God is righteous, and that which stands up within us hungers and thirsts for Him. I was like that. Then I believed in Him, and that which stands up within me was satisfied, and my body was made well, too. I became really happy. Eating peyote is not good. It causes that which stands up within you to suffer.

One Navajo, lacking education but full of appreciation, wrote, "Yes, I have received a New Testament about a couple weeks ago. It is a very wonderful thing I ever get that what I been looking for a long time and thank you for the wonderful book."

Periodically more printings of the New Testament were issued, until by the end of 1967 it had been reprinted seven times and 14,500 copies were in use in hogans and modern homes, in missions and schools, scattered far and wide over the land of The People.

17

Navajo Is "In"

THOSE WHO HAD predicted that a strong trend toward the use of English would eventually obviate the use of Navajo had miscalculated. They had underestimated the innate vitality of a culture and language which were not destined to die out.

Numerically The People were increasing—another important factor to be considered by Indian administrators. By the end of 1967, there were well over one hundred thousand Navajos, and they were increasing at the rate of one thousand a year.

Both in missions and in general educational circles signs of Navajo renaissance began to appear in the mid-fifties. Coincidentally—or relatedly—the movement began to gather force about the time of the publication of the New Testament.

There were, of course, those exponents of Navajo education, like Robert Young, who had never lost faith in the power of bilingual teaching. He had been one of the early advocates of the use of the mother tongue and had on a limited scale proven his principle. But there were other forces at work which would strengthen his hands. Increasingly educators were coming to the conclusion that school dropouts on the reservation, particularly in secondary and higher education, might be due to the fact that English was to many students a second language. It was essentially foreign to most Navajos. Universities which produced teachers for reservation schools were turning their attention to solving the problem at the source.

Immediately upon the publication of the Navajo New Testament there was popular demand among missionaries for instruction in Navajo for themselves. The handwriting was on the wall: the day of the interpreter was passing, for now the Navajos could read the Word of God for themselves. Bible classes and teaching would be in Navajo, for that is what The People wanted.

In 1957 Faye and Faith consented to teach a language course for missionaries, on the condition that it be open to all regardless of denominational affiliation. In the first Navajo Language School held near Gallup, thirty attended, representing twelve groups.

A primary objective of the course was to provide a grasp of conversational Navajo. The missionaries were serious, for they were eager to speak the language. The nine-week course included intensive practice in conversation.

There are times, however, when even missionaries become amused and temporarily lose their serious purpose. One of them at the first language school, Irvy Goossen, remembers such an incident involving a small instructor who was intent upon teaching her students to speak Navajo:

"A group of us were sitting around the table. Faye was at the head of the table teaching the class. Everyone, in turn, was trying to say a few words in Navajo. It was all new, and apparently it sounded awfully funny. I don't know why, but we kept on laughing. Every time someone tried to say something, we laughed. All at once Faye got up, stood behind her chair and said, 'Now, folks, if you aren't going to settle down and start learning, and *quit laughing,* I'm going to get mad!' "

Mr. Goossen "quit laughing" long enough to learn a great deal of Navajo during the course. He had worked for several years with The People, but now he saw the importance of using their language.

Upon leaving the course he visited a new community and spoke to its residents in Navajo. From then on, they spoke to him only in the language, assuming that he was a fluent speaker.

"One time a woman turned around and asked me a question," Mr. Goossen recalled, "and to this day I don't know what she asked me. I asked her to repeat. Instead of making it simpler, she just kept on asking the same question, which I didn't understand. Finally she said in disgust, 'How come you can speak our language to us, and then when we say something to you, you don't understand?' I determined then that this shouldn't happen again."

From that time on he set himself to master the art of speaking Navajo, and he became not only a fluent speaker but a teacher of others. Upon the basis of the lessons which had been used in the Navajo Language Course, he wrote a textbook, *Navajo Made Easier,* now widely used in the teaching of Navajo. In appreciation for the start given him in the practical use of Navajo he dedicated the volume "to Miss Faye Edgerton and Miss Faith Hill."

Mr. Goossen's ability in the language, coupled with his gift for teaching others, has equipped him to fill a strategic post at the University of Northern Arizona. Recognizing the wisdom of using the Indian language in the educational process, administrators are now encouraging study of the language by teachers on the reservation. But qualified instructors at the university level are rare. Irvy Goossen is one of the few who were able to meet the urgent need.

An account featuring the popularity of his Navajo teaching on the campus appeared in the University of Northern Arizona paper, *Lumberjack,* October 11, 1967. It stated in part:

> Navajo, as a subject of formal linguistic study, is experiencing a mild boom in northern Arizona.
>
> So says Irvy Goossen, 43-year-old Canadian-born Mennonite missionary, who after 16 years' residence on the sprawling Reservation north and east of Flagstaff, speaks Navajo like a Navajo.
>
> Goossen this fall is teaching "Conversational Navajo" to more than 100 students at Flagstaff's Northern Arizona University and in classes at Tuba City and Window Rock in Navajoland.
>
> The unusual course is a cooperative venture by NAU and the Northern Arizona Supplementary Education Center (NASEC), an agency which provides special educational services to the more than 50 school districts in the five-county northern Arizona area. . . .
>
> Goossen sees the new course in Navajo as filling a long-standing need, particularly for English-speaking whites who work with Navajos on or off the Reservation. . . .

Like any boom, the current one in Navajo has its problems.

For one thing, Goossen says probably less than half-a-dozen people in the area are qualified to teach the language, and most of them have other demands on their time.

For another, there is no textbook. Because of this, Goossen set to work and wrote one himself—a 280-page, 64-lesson manual entitled "Navajo Made Easier"—and had 700 copies printed last June. "They have gone so fast that I might not have enough copies left for all the students I have this fall," he notes ruefully. . . .

In addition to teaching Navajo as an academic subject, Mr. Goossen has participated in the translation of the Old Testament into Navajo, a live project on the reservation at present. No sooner was the New Testament in use than the Navajos began to express strong desires to see the whole Bible in their language. Faye had spearheaded the revision of Genesis and Exodus, which had been translated by early missionaries. She had checked the translation of Joshua, Ruth, and Jonah, done by later missionaries and Navajos. Mr. Goossen, encouraged by Faye, undertook the responsibility for translating the Psalms. A revised edition of these six books of the Old Testament was published in 1966 in one volume by the American Bible Society.

On leave of absence from his mission to fulfill his commission at the university, Mr. Goossen plans, when released, to help complete the Old Testament translation on which Mr. and Mrs. Warren Davis of Cortez, New Mexico, are currently working.

The stabilized written form of the language, and the growing demand for literature in it, is providing spiritual and psychological security for a tribe which a few years ago was suspended between two worlds—the white man's and the Indian's. The language gap is now being bridged by bilingual education. And The People now have an increasing sense of security because they have an important Book in their own Diné bizaad.

Even some medicine men are beginning to see the advantages enjoyed by Christians who have an intelligent basis for faith. In a hospital recently, a medicine man who was a patient said wistfully to a visiting Navajo evangelist, "You Christians have an advantage—your religion is written in a book."

18

Apache Pioneers

TO SOME Anglo-Americans, Apaches are pictures on postcards. Or they are prehistoric bands of marauding savages. To some they are genuine but picturesque hippies, quaintly constructing their own pinyon-pitch water baskets—just for fun.

The real Apaches of Arizona live in two general groups in the White Mountain and the San Carlos areas. They speak closely related dialects comprising a major language designated as Western Apache.* Linguistically the Apaches are cousins of the Navajos, since both nations belong to the Athapaskan-speaking peoples.

Apaches are hard-working, serious Indians. They are beset by a two-pronged frustration harassing most minority groups: a discomfort arising from a culture-language identity of themselves which separates them from their neighbors. The active Tribal Council is solving many of the cultural and economic problems of the tribe.

* For the relationship of these dialects see Faith Hill's article, "Some Comparisons Between the San Carlos and White Mountain Dialects of Western Apache," in *Studies in the Athapaskan Language* (Berkeley: University of California Press, 1963), pp. 149–54.

The language barrier is less amenable to rapid modification. Even with the efficient intermeshing wheels of tribal and national government machines, people—any linguistic group of people—cannot overnight shift their language gears.

Linguists and missionaries have investigated and analyzed the Apache language, which is structurally similar to Navajo. Differences in social organization and culture between the two Indian nations, however, represent a greater gap than linguistic studies might indicate. Practically, many terms for artifacts and actions are quite different.

Before the Navajo New Testament was finished, Faye and Faith had already thought about Apacheland. Anita would continue with Navajo literacy. Missions had worked among the Apaches for years—but there was no Apache New Testament. The same urge which had produced the Navajo Book was at work within the translators, directed now toward the Apaches.

There were obstacles, however. Faye's heart was "acting up" now and then, and she tired more easily since the big push to get the Navajo Testament to press. But the team possessed one major asset—the endless energy and ambition of a younger partner! If Faye provided the initial vision for the task, Faith was eager to implement the undertaking.

There was one nagging question in Faith's conscientious mind: What about her frail mother, now almost ninety years of age? But "that which stood up" in Mrs. Hill was stronger than her fragile body.

"Of course I will go with thee!" was the response to her daughter when the venture was suggested.

In a letter sent out for Christmas, 1955, was a note stating: "Faye and Faith are looking for an opening in Apacheland. . . ." All they wanted for Christmas was a door ajar, entrance to another land of labor.

While still reading proof on the Navajo New Testament Faye and Faith and a perky little Quaker mother tucked themselves into the Volkswagen and set forth to "prospect," hoping to stake a claim in Apache country.

They acquired a small house trailer and parked it in Globe, Arizona, on the border of the San Carlos Apache Reservation. There they began to make friends with people of the tribe, in order to initiate study of the language. They soon found that even Apaches living near the large town of Globe were speaking their own tongue in their homes. Only when children started to school did they learn English. This confirmed the need for a translation.

During the winter of 1954–1955 a friend observing Mrs. Hill happily tucked in the trailer with the two translators suggested that she write a book entitled *Life Begins at Ninety*. She thoroughly enjoyed the close quarters, and even the adventures of traveling in a trailer. Someone had asked, "How is moving—in a trailer?" She answered, "It's easy— at the packing end. You just stuff some pillows in the cupboards, put heavy things on the floor, and away you go, like a turtle who carries his house on his back."

During the winter Mrs. Hill became ill with bronchial pneumonia. She seemed to recover but was in a weakened condition. In February she quietly went to be with her Lord, whom she had trusted with calm Quaker confidence for most of her ninety years.

Faith wrote, "It is lonesome here without Mother, but she is Home, where there are no moving problems."

As Faye and Faith made Apache friends and gained their confidence, they began to see tokens of encouragement toward their translation task. An influential Apache, a member of the Tribal Council, attended a church which Faye and Faith were visiting. When he discovered their desire, he asked them to write down some hymns in Apache for him and his fellow believers to sing.

"I go to camp meetings where I hear Navajos and Pimas

and other Indians singing in their own languages," he told them, "but we have no hymns written in Apache."

It was premature, the translators told him, for them to undertake the translation of hymns, for their knowledge of Apache was limited. But with his help they would try.

Within a short time the translators had written down phonetically the words of several hymns. Apache Christians began to sing them, and all were overjoyed with the results. They were especially delighted to see their language for the first time in readable written form.

Hymn singing proved to be the entering wedge for the translation of the New Testament. As the number of hymns grew, the translators' knowledge of the language increased until they were able to undertake actual translation. And the Apaches' morale was boosted by seeing their language on paper.

Anxious to live closer to the Apaches on the reservation in order to gain fluency in the language, they made trips, testing possibilities. Housing in the rugged Indian country was not easily available. The terrain was mountainous, and the Apaches lived in small, scattered groups.

Once they wrote, "The road crew at White River was away for the weekend, so beds were available for us at the Broken Arrow Hotel." Another time they noted, "We stayed at Show Low last night ad the next day looked up a colony of Apaches who live at a sawmill there." At one isolated area they found a colony of eight families who invited them to "come and park their trailer."

In 1956 the problem of where to live in Apacheland was temporarily shelved, as they became busily involved in the final proofreading of the Navajo New Testament and the plans for its dedication and distribution. They were not able to return to Apache country until December.

Their search for a good location ended at an asbestos mine, where the owner gave them a room in one of his buildings and permission to work on the language with his Indian employees. This proved to be an ideal situation for learning the language, and a center from which they made contacts on both reservations.

They were immediately able to help Apaches, employed at the mine, with moral and spiritual problems. Much of the money earned was spent on drinking, and alcoholism was ruining many homes.

One Sunday morning a young woman, Celena, came to talk with the translators about her desperate condition. Both she and her husband were drinking heavily, but they honestly wanted release from the habit. Their lives were being wrecked, and they sought help.

Celena and her husband knelt in prayer in the translators' room, asking God for salvation and for deliverance from the habit of drinking.

"God granted their petitions," Faith wrote, "for they were from that time completely freed from alcoholism. They were never even tempted to drink again. We have seldom seen such a total break with the old life."

Celena became a valuable translation helper. She was eager for the Word of God in her language, and she faithfully assisted in the task which amounted to a Bible education for her.

Through the translators' friendship with Celena, an invitation was extended to them to live in her mother's camp on the San Carlos reservation. Grateful for this opportunity to live in an Apache camp, they wrote: "Celena's mother is letting us build a 12' × 14' cabin near hers in San Carlos. The Lord is enabling us to keep it within our means— lumber at a nearby planing mill for less than half price, a door salvaged from the 'dump,' and used windows. We are happy to think that when we are through with the cabin, it will go on serving this Apache family who have given freely of their time for translation work."

Early in the Apache translation Faye and Faith received valuable help from a veteran Lutheran missionary, Dr. Francis Uplegger, who had pioneered among the Apaches. Faye wrote of him: "Now ninety years old, he is a most gracious gentleman, still somewhat active in the work as he preaches almost every Sunday in Apache." In the early days of his experience, when deciding upon a biblical term for the name of God, he very wisely chose to use the name of a corresponding Apache deity, The One from Whom Life Comes. Because of this felicitous choice there was never any problem with the concept of a "white man's God" among the Apaches; He was *their* God.

Terms for king and kingdom posed problems, as they had in Navajo. When probing for a word for the latter expression, the translators asked an Apache, "How would you say that the tribal chairman is in charge of the people of San Carlos?"

"We might say," suggested the helper, "they are in his hand." The phrase "those who are in God's hand" was accepted by all and was incorporated into the Apache New Testament.

Translation helpers cooperating on the manuscript were eager to have the Word speak strongly in their language, and they were unselfish in their help. One woman, enthusiastic about the Apache translation, said about hearing the gospel in English, "It goes into my *head* in English, but it goes down into my *heart* in Apache."

She was more fortunate than some; there were many monolingual Apaches who did not possess a dual language system. It was primarily for these that the Word was being prepared.

In the summer of 1958 a seminar on the Athapaskan languages of North America was held in Norman, Oklahoma, under the direction of Faye's friend and mentor, Dr. Harry

Hoijer. Faye participated, undertaking a full study of sentence types in Western Apache. She took valuable months out of her translation schedule the following year to prepare her investigation for publication. Titled "The Tagmemic Analysis of Sentence Structure in Western Apache,"* it was a thorough treatment of the grammar of the language as expressed through its sentence patterns. Her diligent labor was rewarded by the compliments of her linguistic leaders, Drs. Pike and Hoijer.

While Faye was called upon from time to time for linguistic jobs and other duties, Faith kept steadily at the Apache translation. She made trips to Cedar Creek, on the White River reservation, to check the translation with speakers of that area. A trailer house was set up on the property of friends for convenient living while she, sometimes accompanied by Faye, was there.

In 1965 the Apache New Testament was ready for the press. Again, as for the Navajo Testament, Faith carefully typed long hours for months to produce a perfect copy of the peculiar script for the American Bible Society.

"Excuse me for crying," said an old Apache woman as she clasped her copy of the New Testament affectionately. "When they told me that God's Word would be printed in my language I never believed I would live to see the day."

Apaches up and down the beautiful White River Valley were proudly showing and sharing their new Book. It was an especially happy day for those who had worked in the little trailer or in the one-room cabin—or sometimes in hot summer weather in an open brush arbor—to finish the Apache translation. The beautifully bound book was a prized possession of these, and many others.

Soon after The Book's publication in 1966, Bible Trans-

* *Studies in the Athapaskan Language, op. cit.,* pp. 102–48.

lation Day was declared officially in Washington, D.C., with an impressive ceremony in the new Senate building on September 30. Appropriately, the Apache New Testament became the *pièce de résistance* of the important occasion. Britton Goode, a member of the Apache Tribal Council and a staunch Christian, was asked to go to the Capitol to present the Scriptures in his language to his country's highest officials. His wife, Marie, dressed in tribal costume, accompanied him.

With deliberate dignity Mr. Goode made a speech as he presented The Book. He said: "Long ago we Indians used to carry bows and arrows with us wherever we went. When we would lie down at night our bows and arrows were beside us. When we would sit down to eat we would lay them beside us.

"Now we do not carry bows and arrows any more. But we Christian Apaches carry our Bibles. I am glad that now I have the New Testament in my own language."

Congressman Ben Reifel from South Dakota, participating in the ceremony, was happy to own his Sioux ancestry. He told of the Sioux Bible, which his mother loved, and presented the Goodes with a copy of his mother's Sioux hymnbook. In conclusion, Representative Reifel said, "I am sure that if my mother had not been a Christian, I would not be in Congress today."

Senator Fred R. Harris of Oklahoma was more than perfunctorily happy to be included in the ceremony. A lover of Indians, he was especially fond of one—his wife—a full-blooded Cherokee. His appropriate remarks, sparkling with characteristic wit, illuminated the otherwise dignified occasion.

After the ceremony a copy of the Testament was presented to an aide for President Johnson. With dignity and perceptible pride, Mr. Goode took time to turn to a passage, John 14:6, and read it clearly and emphatically in his own Apache tongue to the listening aide.

Later in the day copies were presented to other Congressmen, including Senator Everett Dirksen from Illinois. He was pleased. With a smile, he intoned in his lilting rhetoric: "They just handed me a copy of the Bible translated into the Apache language. Not being an Apache scholar who pursues the study of the language, I am in no position to evaluate the work. But I do believe it is a marvelous thing that the great Good Book will ultimately have been translated into every spoken and written language. What a wealth of comfort and inspiration will be opened up to millions of people. I congratulate you on this effort."

19

Unfadable Faye

TIME: March 26, 1964.
PLACE: Translation Workshop, Ixmiquilpan, Mexico.
OCCASION: Surprise party for Faye on her seventy-fifth birthday.
PARTICIPANTS: A family affair—fifty admiring fellow Wycliffe translators.
POET LAUREATE: Dr. Robert Longacre, translation consultant.

> This is the chronicle of unfadable Faye
> Compounding her strength on every birthday:
>
> Faye Edgerton at seventy-five
> Said, "It's great to be alive;
> I'm working hard and far from spent—
> Will start my third New Testament."
>
> Faye Edgerton at seventy-six
> To her labor bravely sticks.

Faye Edgerton at seventy-seven:
Hardest worker this side of heaven.

Faye Edgerton at seventy-eight:
Translating full time and feeling great.

Faye Edgerton at seventy-nine:
Translator-consultant, feeling fine.

At eighty she was heard to say:
"I *may* be getting old *some day*."

At eighty-five, quite fresh in heart,
In Timbuctoo she made a start.
The director said, "Don't send more men;
Edgerton does the work of *ten!*"

At ninety, with her accustomed fire,
She spurned the thought she should retire.

At one hundred, still unbent,
She finished her twelfth New Testament.

At one hundred and ten she began to complain!
"I'm stiff in the joints and I feel the strain."

At one hundred and twenty she began to slow
(Only working half a day, you know).

Sometime later—just when I can't say—
She had her own "Translation Day."

Always "fresh in heart," Faye was often the center of
attraction and admiration in a Wycliffe gathering. At the
Translation Workshop in Mexico, where she was learning
the latest techniques for checking Indian translations, her
younger friends were delighted for an appropriate occasion to fete her. Until the subject of birthdays was mentioned, no one thought of Faye's age; she was ageless, as
young as any in the crowd. Her merry chuckle and her
blue eyes that twinkled when she was amused made her
always welcome.

"It was all a real surprise!" Faye wrote. She had not told

anyone—and had almost forgotten the day herself. But her thoughtful partner, Faith, had written one of the friends at the workshop, who then organized the party. One reason for Faye's almost forgetting the day was that she had been busy as consultant at the workshop and had "worked six hours checking First Peter. . . ." Six hours, working under the direction of chief consultant John Beekman, was a solid day's work, with time only for a lunch break. Faye was as diligent as her boss, and the birthday had almost passed unnoticed.

"I can hardly believe it—" Faye said in a letter describing the affair, "but the calendar doesn't lie!" In retrospect of her seventy-five years she continued, "The Lord has been very gracious to me. I thank Him for bringing me to Himself, and for letting me be a missionary—even *me*, 'that frivolous Faye Edgerton'! It has been a really thrilling and fascinating life, and I wouldn't change it—except to wish that I had been more faithful sometimes."

Hours of relaxation at Ixmiquilpan were treasured and memorable. Most of the three months was filled by intensive seminars on Bible translation or actual consultation with translators on problems encountered in turning the Scriptures into neat, meaningful Indian phrases. At the particular session Faye attended, teams from fourteen tribes in Mexico and the United States participated. By listening to "back translations," anglicized versions of the Indian wording "played back" into an intelligible English equivalent, one could compare the rendering with the original Greek New Testament. By such a process consultants were often able to guide translators into making dynamic, powerful Indian versions, producing the same type of impact upon the tribal readers as the original version did upon the early Christians. And the strength of first-century Christianity was being reproduced in tribal groups where such translations were read.

The leader of the dynamic translation movement at the Wycliffe Workshop was John Beekman, a translator who had himself produced an idiomatic Indian New Testament for the Chol tribe of southern Mexico. With several other Wycliffe workers, he had pioneered in the language, reducing it to writing and eventually producing the Chol New Testament. Through it a strong indigenous church of thousands of Chol Indians had been born, with literate Chol leaders bearing full responsibility for their own organization.

In the early days of his tribal work John tramped the trails of the roadless, mountainous area, checking the translation in distant villages and teaching Indians to read it. The arduous labors further weakened his ailing heart. By the time the Chol New Testament was finished in 1955. John was faced with the alternatives of open heart surgery or premature death. He and his wife decided that he should risk the operation, which would replace a failing aorta valve with a plastic one. Heart surgery was in its infancy, and guarantees for recovery were only a hope. John's surgeon told the Beekmans that if all went well, he might live five years.

By 1960 the plastic valve was still functioning so efficiently that John was given the challenge of organizing a translation workshop in Mexico. Here his valuable knowledge concerning Bible translation could be shared with translators who would come from various areas of the world for sessions of three months each. Thus his strength could be conserved and the cause of Bible translation enriched.

By mid-1968, John was still training translators, and he had never missed a session at the workshop. He had almost forgotten about the doctor's five-year prediction. There was, however, one constant and audible reminder of the miracle: a loud ticking sound emanating from his person, even when his mouth was closed.

The obvious ticktock mystifies strangers, but it furnishes no end of amusement for John, who despite his ailment is something of a rascal and enjoys a good joke.

John and Faye, already good friends, spent hours together dreaming of the future and planning for workshops in the United States, including Alaska, where several Wycliffe teams were working, and Canada. In their projections they talked as if they would live forever! Neither seemed to consider their heart conditions—Faye was now taking "heart pills."

For Faye the future was full: completion of the Apache New Testament, revision of the Navajo, and assistance to her colleagues working in tribes in North America. Long experience now sharpened by new techniques uniquely fitted her to give valuable consultation.

When the Apache Testament was finally completed in 1965, an unexpected bonus was awarded Faye. Faith had been asked to conduct a literacy workshop at Wycliffe's language school in England. Faye was tired and needed a rest. What better treatment than a trip with her partner to England, with no responsibilities for a summer? At first Faye flatly rejected Faith's suggestion. It would cost too much, and there were many projects needing attention on *this* side of the Atlantic.

Faith argued, "But you've always said that when you retire you want to travel. Yet you pray that you may be able to keep working to the end. So why not travel *now?*"

In the end Faith won, and to the satisfaction of both partners, they enjoyed a refreshingly chilly summer in England.

From the moment they embarked on the *Queen Mary,* every hour of the voyage was pure bliss. "It was calm all the way—we scarcely knew we were on the sea!" And the excellent food, the stimulation of making new friends, and the temporary freedom from working long hours revived the tired translators.

"But it is *cold!*" they wrote upon arriving in England. "It is like November!" With hot-water bottles for their beds at night and extra sweaters for day wear, they enjoyed living in the exciting land of their forefathers. Faye was particularly anxious to "see everything." Before the Wycliffe school started they therefore spent several days sightseeing and even managed a quick trip to Scotland.

Back in London the Yankee sightseers hurried to their assignment at the Wycliffe school. After a full summer of work for Faith, in which her partner became somewhat involved, the travelers made a hurried trip to other parts of England and the Continent.

"We enjoyed two days on the west coast of England in the home of Stuart Hine, translator of the English version of the song 'How Great Thou Art,' and father of one of our Wycliffe members, Sonia Hine," Faye wrote. "Our first contact with him was several years ago when we wrote him, asking for permission to translate the song into Navajo, and to publish the music score."

In France Faye received news from the States, the only sad note in an otherwise perfect trip: her sister Goldie had suddenly died in Texas. Faye was happy that she had seen her the previous April. Goldie was at that time the last living member of the close-knit Nebraska family.

Back in Farmington, revitalized and ready to work, Faye and Faith put away their souvenirs. Soon they prepared for another type of travel.

"Our friends are calling us 'wanderers' these days. The Lord has surely 'preserved' our 'going out' and our 'coming in' during the past months," Faye told friends as she reviewed the past and planned for the future.

The year 1966 was crowded with challenging tasks involving far-flung travel. After the distribution of the newly published Apache New Testament in Arizona, with scarcely time to repack the faithful Volkswagen, the partners prepared for a trip to Seattle, from where they would fly to Alaska. Faye had been requested to consult with fellow translator Don Webster, who with his Eskimo cotranslator, Roy Amaogak, was completing the Inupiat New Testament. Faith was to assist Wycliffe members, including the Shinen family living on St. Lawrence Island just off the coast of Siberia, as literacy consultant.

"Because of the time change," Faye wrote back to friends, "we arrived in Fairbanks five minutes before we left Seattle!"

Six miles out of Fairbanks was the Wycliffe base, "a lovely spot, a clearing in the forest of tall firs and gleaming white birch trees." Here Faye spent the summer in beautiful surroundings, checking the Testament which had been the lifetime dream of the Eskimo translator. He had been born at Point Barrow and for many years had been a faithful Presbyterian pastor to his own people. Although himself bilingual, he had longed to see the Bible in his language, and had worked alone on the project for many years. Later, he was delighted to collaborate with Wycliffe members in completing the task.

Faye wrote: "Eskimo culture is very different from that of the Jews in Palestine. Eskimos have never seen sheep or swine, a cultivated field, or a marketplace. The root of the words used for 'generations' and 'descendants' is the same as that of the word for the long rope from the lead dog to the sled. All the other dogs are harnessed to the same rope."

Earlier, when she had made a trip to Wainwright, she had written: "The sun went down about eleven o'clock and arose again before one. Not a shrub or tree can be found on the Arctic coast, but long grass covers the wet, soggy ground in some places. The rain and melting snow cannot sink into the ground because of the perma-frost. A hole in this makes a natural deep freeze for the caribou, fish, seal, walrus and whale meat, the Eskimos' chief food. This 'refrigerator' also holds ice cut from the lakes to be melted for drinking water. You enter your 'deep freeze' by means of a ladder in Eskimoland."

Faye enjoyed hearing the Eskimo language and working with Roy and Don in the final stages of the Testament.

"I had fun listening to long Eskimo words," she said. "I found one that had *forty-nine letters* in it! It is a complex word, with the root in the middle and 'things' added to both sides of it." She compared it to Navajo, in which parts of long words are added "at the end."

At home again in Farmington, Faye was delighted when she heard the good news in 1967 that the Inupiat New Testament was being printed. She was saddened, however, to hear in early 1968 of the sudden death of Roy Amaogak, her Eskimo friend.

"But I'm so *glad* that the Lord spared him until he finished the Testament!" she exclaimed.

20

"Grandma Has to Go to School"

THE "SCHOOL" was a one-room cabin under the pines at the foot of Mount Eldon in Flagstaff. Every morning at nine on the dot, the "class" met, a class composed of Jonathan Ekstrom, translator of the Hopi New Testament, Elsie Polacca, faithful Hopi helper, and Faye Edgerton, consultant. It was the summer of 1967, and the Hopi New Testament was being checked for publication.

Elsie was living with relatives, including a grandson, just

across the pine woods from Faye's cabin. Jonathan, who lived with his family in another corner of the woods, called for Elsie each morning in his carryall. A playmate of her grandson, observing the daily ritual, asked, "Where does your Grandma go?"

"Grandma has to go to school" was the matter-of-fact reply.

"Yes," laughed Elsie good-naturedly when she heard the remark, "I have to go to school—and Miss Edgerton is my teacher!"

As the translation trio kept regular hours, week after week, it was a type of "teach each other" class, as they all worked toward solutions of difficult phrases or expressions.

"Indeed I am going to school!" chuckled Elsie later, commenting on the hard work involved in producing a good translation. "I'm old now, but still I can learn a lot of things that the Lord teaches us."

"But Miss Edgerton is improving her education, too!" Elsie added.

It was true. With a tableful of versions and commentaries, and with an intelligent Hopi woman at her side, she was learning new truths from the Bible as well as fascinating facts about Hopi life and thinking.

A practical Christian, Elsie had comments that were always helpful. Reflecting on the verses in Romans 12 concerning the treatment of enemies, she said, "I like this Scripture because it tells us what not to do, and what to do. We would say in Hopi, if an enemy is hungry, if he is thirsty, feed him and give him something to drink. Doing that you will make him ashamed of what he has done to you. We Indians like to eat a lot. If somebody comes that doesn't like me, and I feed him good things, he'll be happy to eat.

"Or maybe somebody needs our help. Go and help him. And if anybody comes to your house, welcome him, receive him gladly. Now the Hopi woman—if you go to her house and knock—she won't just stand there, or she won't come out to you. She'll say, 'Come in. Sit down.' That's the way we were taught. We were taught to welcome people.

"Of course now it's kind of dangerous because they say you mustn't welcome every stranger, so it's kind of hard. But where I came from, we always welcomed people.

"When we go to the home of some of our friends—we are not enemies—these people walk outside and talk to you outside. At first when I saw that I thought they were rude, but that's their own way of doing it. The Hopis aren't that way. They say, 'Come in.' "

Elsie's observations, particularly regarding customs, were valuable, for she had adjusted to four racial groups and had learned their languages: her own Hopi, neighboring Navajo, Spanish, and English. Affable and relaxed, Elsie was the translator's dream of an ideal helper. She was frank to reject a rendering which was not good Hopi but always ready with helpful suggestions for substitutes.

In commenting on Paul's teaching of many members but one body, Elsie said, "We are all like a chain, connected one to another. Each one of us has something to do. If it's only to sweep the floor of our church, I'm willing to do it for the Lord."

Faye would sometimes smile in agreement with Elsie's comments, and sometimes she would make a notation in a little book, saying, "That gives me an idea for our Navajo revision! That's *good*, Elsie!"

Faye was consumed with a desire to incorporate all of the good ideas which she had gleaned from Mexico, and from Eskimos and Hopis, into an improved Navajo version.

One gem which she noted was the Hopi for Second Timothy 2:17, "And their word will eat as doth a canker." A canker turned out to be a carbuncle, and the Hopi word for carbuncle was "an anthill sore." "Their words will become like an anthill sore," said the Hopi verse.

When seeking the best expressions for Persons of the Trinity, Elsie was helpful in making comparisons with Hopi leaders. She often drew upon the experience of her father, who was an honored chief among his people and who earned the respect of many white leaders as well. A troublesome phrase in Jude, "denying the only Lord God, and our Lord Jesus Christ," turned out in Hopi to say: "They disowned God, the only Chief, and Jesus Christ, our Controller."

Elsie loved to reminisce about her mother, a devoted Christian, who had told her, "Now you have to learn to pray for your own children. I'm not going to be living all the time. You have to learn to pray."

"I want to follow the Lord," Elsie continued, "and I want to teach my children, and my grandchildren, and my great-grandchildren. I have fifty-three grandchildren—and one on the way. I had ten children to begin with, and that's why there are so many grandchildren. Now the great-grand-children are coming, too!

"But I don't think that I will live to see my great-great-grandchildren, like my Dad did!"

21

"Write It!"

EVERY HOUR which could be spared from other duties Faye spent on the Navajo revision. When The Book had been first published, she said that in ten years it should be revised by The People themselves. Through the widespread use of the volume she had received many valuable reactions and even suggestions for improvement in wording.

There were some, however, like Pastor Little Man, who

were satisfied with the Word of God as it was. These would need to be tactfully convinced that improvement was possible.

Most of all, Faye had learned much from her colleagues as she had guided them into vigorous ways of expressing God's thoughts in other tribal languages. Old Bible gems were continually reflecting new shining prisms of light for her own soul in the process. These nuances of expression would in many instances, she felt, enrich the Navajo text.

Roger's help in revision was a valuable asset, for he was eager to search for ways of strengthening the Navajo Scriptures. The first months of 1967 were devoted to intensive work on reviewing the Pauline Epistles, making necessary changes. As they endeavored to clarify obscure passages, sometimes they would discover a beautiful word or expression, a happy solution to a word puzzle. At such times a light would flash in Roger's black eyes as he exclaimed, *"Aniléh*—write it!" His intonation said, "That's *exactly* it—write it quick before we lose it!"

Several times a day, after "think" sessions, Faye would hear those heartening words, a translator's reward! She would write, as Roger thought. This was the division of labor agreed upon, although Roger was proficient at writing as well as reading his own language.

As book after book was updated, Faye cherished the hope of finishing the whole revision by summertime. Typical interruptions prevented, however, and when they were well launched into the project, it was time to go and join the Hopi committee.

In the evenings in Flagstaff after working with the Hopi team all day, Faye would sometimes muster energy for the Navajo revision. Christians living nearby, such as Pastor Little Man and his friends, would help her. Others were also recruited for the task, for there were readers of the Testament who caught the vision of a revitalized text.

When the Hopi project was completed in October, Faye

turned her total attention toward termination of the new Navajo version.

The chill nights promised an early, hard winter. By November there were snow flurries, and December brought the Big Snow which spread death and devastation over the reservation.

The snow began to mount higher and higher around the little cabin, and the roads to the campground were completely obliterated. The little Volkswagen became a white motionless mound in front of a cabin that threatened to be suffocated by the growing snowpile.

Faye was concerned for Navajos stranded on the reservation, cut off from any source of supplies. She thought of her many friends in Cornfields Valley, and Crystal, and Fort Defiance. Many were suffering.

Her old friend, Grace Segar Davis, now a widow but faithfully serving Christ and her own people in a mission at Indian Wells, wrote an account of the storm:

The storm hit December 12th. The community carders had just started the carding and spinning of wool, also the weaving project for the women. All activities were stopped. The flocks of sheep had to stay in corrals for days. The horses and cattle went into the wooded hills to sheltered places. We watched the snow piling up, going into drifts. Grass and vegetation were covered. I would have thoroughly enjoyed the snow had it not been for the fact our people in the out-of-the-way places back in the hills were suffering.

The sun finally came out after a week of hiding behind clouds. For days we did not see any life on the roads. It was a strange sensation not to see vehicles which we are all so used to—no mail going or coming for two weeks.

The planes started flying over as soon as the sky cleared, dropping food and hay near homes. Then the helicopters also came. They brought food for both people and beasts. The sick were flown out. A woman in labor was taken to the highway in a wagon and was taken to the hospital 35 miles distant in the storm. Two families were flown out to the town of

Holbrook, leaving the flock of sheep corraled. Some of the sheep survived the ten days of being shut in.

A Christian woman said, "We all realize now how helpless we are. With all the inventions, we have taken life for granted, thinking we were able to deal with any emergency which might arise. With one sweep of God's Hand we were all laid low and found how helpless we are when God acts."

We are thankful for the help given by the people who sent in the airplanes and helicopters. We are thankful to Christian friends who remembered us in prayer.

Eventually the snowplows chewed their way through the white mountain and the campground where Faye and Faith were snowed in. Friends extricated the Volkswagen, and by Christmas time the adventurers were on their way back to Farmington.

It was good to be home.

A pile of another kind had accumulated at home base. It was a high heap of heartwarming greetings and letters from friends far and wide. As soon as the messages were read and enjoyed, Faye was eager to resume the task which now occupied her thoughts.

And Roger was there at her side, ready to tell her to "write it!"

22

Still Writing?

THERE HAD BEEN no warning of the stroke which partially paralyzed Faye on the early morning of December 29, 1967. During the five weeks in the hospital she recovered well, and she returned home in January. She was able to consult with Roger and Faith, who were now continuing the work of revision. Faith had picked up Faye's pen and was listening for the welcome signal to "write it!"

At times Faye said, as they worked on hard verses in Peter's Epistles, "I'm tired, I'm too tired to *think* . . ." and she would excuse herself and lie down to rest.

"She helped us on *these*," Roger remembered, moving his muscular brown hand over a much revised page of Navajo script.

"These" were phrases for which Faye had offered good suggestions: "The sufferings of Christ and the glory that should follow," and the "gospel sent down from heaven . . . which things the angels also desire to look into."

She had thought of a better way of saying in Navajo, "a light that shineth in a dark place, until the day dawn, and the Day Star arise in your hearts."

"Here is where she helped a *lot*"—a verse she had emphasized—Roger remembered.

Too moved to read it, he only pointed to the Navajo version of Second Peter 1:15: "Moreover, I will endeavor that ye may be able after my decease to have these things always in remembrance."

When Dorothy heard of Faye's illness she came from her home at Yellow-at-the-Edge-of-the-Woods to see her friend. They had a hilarious evening, going through old picture albums and recalling the days in Pine Springs and Crystal, and the snow drifting in through the cracks onto their beds in Window Rock . . .

Now Dorothy had sold the beautiful Navajo jewelry inherited from her mother, and some of the family sheep, to build a small church on the yellow land. It was not far from the path where in the moonlight she had first knelt and prayed to the Good Shepherd.

The little cement-block building was a truly indigenous church, the kind that Faye had envisioned. She was happy to hear of the progress being made, of Dorothy's efforts to reach old people still wearing knotted hair and heavy turquoise ornaments, and the young people home from school.

"My brother Joe can read the Navajo Testament well!" Dorothy said proudly. The church had become a family project. Faye was delighted with the news.

Other Navajo friends and many Wycliffe colleagues phoned or wrote when they heard of Faye's illness.

Dr. Kenneth L. Pike, busy with linguistic lectures at the University of Michigan, wrote a concerned letter, saying in conclusion:

> May the Lord help you to get better—and work again on the Navajo revision. What a tremendous inspiration you have been to us all! Recently I told Robbins [director of Wycliffe's Mexico branch] I hoped that at 70 I could get back and tackle another translation myself, dropping all of this other folderal. Your example encourages us all to think that perhaps it could be done.

Translator of the Mixteco New Testament in Mexico and a distinguished linguist, Pike had always been an unapologetic fan of Faye Edgerton. She had often been embarrassed by his public praise of her accomplishments. His wife, Evelyn, often said with a giggle, "How do any of us Wycliffe folks *ever* stand a chance of retiring—with Faye Edgerton around!"

On February 26 Faye's heart was failing, and she had to return to the hospital. For several days she was in a coma, but she rallied on the morning of March 1. The doctor marveled at her surprising vitality.

Hearing that Faye was back in the hospital, Dorothy

came again on March 4, "to stay three days and help." She stood for hours by Faye's side, stroking her hand and making her as comfortable as possible. She helped the nurses, some of whom were Navajo. They were also concerned about their small patient.

It was nearing midnight. Outside it was cold but clear. The morning star was not yet visible, but clustered in constellations, other stars shivered in the dark overhead. They hung low in the sky, close to the cliff above the San Juan River.

Inside, in the quiet hospital room, Faye was sleepy. Beginning to doze, she licked her thumb and "turned pages." Then she "wrote."

"She kept writing, and writing, like this—" and Dorothy went through the subconscious motions.

Suddenly Faye stopped writing and looked up, awake and alert. Opening her blue eyes wide, she asked, "Who?"

She reached out her hand as if to greet someone.

"Then she smiled—a *beautiful* smile," Dorothy said.

The two-hour memorial service was "more like a fellowship than a funeral," just as the Navajo pastor in charge had said. By Navajo radio broadcasts, word had spread quickly across the reservation, and Faye's Indian friends came from far and near—from Flagstaff and Ganado and Pine Springs and Apacheland.

"Our sister is not here—she has passed into the heavens and is *with Christ!*" exclaimed blind Geronimo in a dynamic sermon which lasted longer than he had planned. He had even consulted his Braille watch midway—but had ignored its message!

Roger read the Scripture loud and clear in Navajo, stopping and struggling briefly from time to time. Controlling his emotions, he bravely concluded the long passage.

Sheppy Martine, the ex-medicine man, expressed his appreciation for The Book "our sister gave us in our language" —in an eloquent, half-hour sermon in Navajo!

"Faye would have loved nothing better!" a friend remarked.

Words of eulogy were few, but they were forceful; the focus of the "fellowship" was on the Word of God. That, too, was what Faye would have wanted.

It was beginning to snow in Albuquerque the following day when others—mostly non-Navajo friends and relatives —gathered in a little chapel for an English language farewell to Faye. Goldie's son and daughter were there, a nephew and niece who had fondly followed "Auntie Faye's missionary journeys."

It had been almost forty-four years since her first train trip to the town bordering Navajo country. The conductor's "All aboard" had cut short her visit with Indian women weaving rugs near the waiting room.

Now there was no hurry. And a small, tired body had time to rest.

But "that which stood up" in Faye, that which kept her working to the end as she had wanted it, was probably busy, standing up straighter and stronger than ever.

Perhaps she was looking into the Book of Life with a curious angel at her side, perhaps even helping him write something—in a script suspiciously resembling an Athapaskan alphabet.

But surely she was telling him how beautifully God had said it in Navajo!